NO-GRI[D]

SURVIVAL PROJECTS

The 1000-Day Blueprint for a Self-Sufficient Life

Practical Solutions & Key Techniques to Achieve Food and Energy Independence and Protect Your Family Through Any Crisis

Jonathan Hyle

Table of Contents

Introduction

Adopting the off-grid lifestyle is a transformative journey, a move away from the conventional towards a life of self-sufficiency and connection with nature.

This lifestyle choice involves a comprehensive shift in living, from disconnecting from public utilities to relying on sustainable sources and adopting a mindset of environmental stewardship. It's a path that demands not only careful planning and consideration but also a deep understanding of one's motivations.

Embracing the Off-Grid Lifestyle: What to Expect

Choosing an off-grid lifestyle is a significant, life-altering decision. It requires a fundamental shift in daily living, where energy independence becomes crucial. You'll explore alternative energy sources such as solar, wind, or hydroelectric systems and learn to harness and store energy efficiently. Water management becomes a proactive task, often involving rainwater harvesting or well drilling. Food production shifts to a self-sustaining cycle where you engage directly with the land to grow your food and potentially raise livestock. Waste management adopts the principles of reduce, reuse, and recycle, turning waste into a resource. Shelter and infrastructure involve building homes that are in harmony with the environment, often using sustainable materials and methods. Despite the perception of isolation, community building remains essential, fostering bonds, sharing knowledge, and creating a support network.

Understanding Your Motivation: Aligning with Your Goals

Your journey into off-grid living should align with your personal goals, whether they be environmental stewardship, self-sufficiency, financial freedom, escaping consumerism, or a deeper connection with nature. This book guides you through these various facets, offering practical advice and real-life examples to help you build a life that's not only sustainable but deeply fulfilling.

"No Grid Survival Projects" will be your guide and a dependable companion on your journey to a self-sufficient life. It will provide you with the tools, knowledge, and inspiration to successfully transition to and thrive in an off-grid lifestyle.

Through its pages, you'll discover a new way of living that's both challenging and rewarding, offering a deeper connection to the world around you. Embark on this journey with us, and transform the way you live, one sustainable step at a time.

Chapter 1:

Fundamentals of Off-Grid Independence

Assessing Your Needs for Self-Sufficiency

The quest for self-sufficiency is an increasingly popular pursuit, driven by a desire for greater independence and resilience.

You stand at the threshold of a life-altering experience, one that rekindles your bond with the simpler rhythms of life. But where to begin? The key lies in understanding your essential needs.

Every journey into off-grid living is unique, tailored to individual needs and circumstances. Begin by evaluating the essentials: food, water, energy, and shelter. How much food will your family require? What are your water needs for drinking, cooking, and hygiene? Consider your energy usage – how much electricity do you consume daily? And let's not forget shelter – what kind of living space will sustain you and your loved ones comfortably?

This assessment is your first step towards self-reliance. It's about understanding not just what you need to survive, but what you need to thrive. Remember, off-grid living isn't about sacrificing comfort; it's about finding balance and harmony with nature. You're not just preparing for a life off the grid; you're preparing for a life of freedom and fulfillment.

As you analyze your needs, recognize that this is merely the commencement of a greater adventure. Your off-grid path is a promise of perpetual learning, evolving, and connecting. Approach each phase of this expedition with eagerness and positivity. Welcome to your new chapter of self-reliance!

The Importance of Self-Sufficiency in Emergency Situations

In an ever-changing world where the unexpected has become the norm, the value of self-sufficiency in emergency situations is immeasurable. Imagine the peace of mind that comes from knowing you are prepared for any eventuality, be it natural disasters, power outages, or societal disruptions.

Self-sufficiency equips you with the skills and resources to stand resilient in the face of crises. It means having your own reliable sources of food, water, and energy, and the knowledge to utilize them effectively. This independence ensures that you and your family remain secure and comfortable, even when external systems fail.

By cultivating self-sufficiency, you are not just preparing for emergencies; you are empowering yourself to take control of your well-being. This proactive approach transforms fear into confidence, enabling you to tackle challenges head-on with a calm and prepared mindset.

In times of uncertainty, self-sufficiency is your safety net. It's about being one step ahead, ready to face whatever comes your way. In this journey, you'll learn that the greatest security comes from within – from the skills you develop and the preparations you make.

Developing A Survival Mindset: Mental Preparedness and Adaptability

Enter a world where unpredictability is the norm, and ordinary life is transformed into something extraordinary. Resilience, adaptability, and good decision-making become your unwavering pillars in this survival mindset, equipping you not only for extreme situations but also for the journey of a lifetime.

Learn to equip yourself with an arsenal of psychological tools to cope with challenges. Deep breathing, mindfulness, and meditation become your shields against stress, helping you remain calm and in control. Cognitive flexibility is your superpower, allowing you to change thoughts and reshape strategies effortlessly. Positive visualization charts the path to success, increasing your mental resilience with each imagined victory.

Cultivate a survival mindset and learn from every experience. View every challenge as an opportunity to innovate and excel, as a chance for continuous improvement. Engage in regular mental exercises, such as problem-solving and scenario planning, to sharpen your mind. Think of it as a game where reusing objects and improvising solutions are the winning moves.

What about in stressful situations? The ability to make sound decisions sets you apart. You learn to set priorities, assess risks, and make choices that matter. Adaptive decision-making is your strategy for success, adapting to new information and circumstances—it's about making the right decisions at the right time.

Set goals and celebrate each victory. Recognize your strengths as badges of honor. A strong social support network provides security and connection, bolstering your mental resilience.

In short, with resilience, adaptability, and a passion for learning, you are well-prepared to conquer the unknown, handling it with empowerment and confidence. Welcome to your journey towards off-grid independence!"

Legal Basics for Off-Grid Living

Embracing an off-grid lifestyle involves not only practical considerations but also a clear understanding of the legal aspects that come with living independently of traditional utilities and infrastructure. Navigating the legal landscape is crucial for ensuring a smooth and lawful off-grid experience.

Land Use and Zoning Regulations

Understanding the land use and zoning regulations in your chosen area is foundational for off-grid living.

- **Zoning Laws:** Zoning regulations define how land can be used and the types of structures that are allowed. Research the zoning laws in your chosen location to ensure that off-grid living is permitted and to understand any restrictions.
- **Land Use Permits:** In some areas, obtaining a land use permit may be necessary for certain off-grid activities. This could include building structures, installing alternative energy systems, or engaging in agriculture. Be aware of the permit requirements and application processes.
- **Rural vs. Urban Zoning:** Rural areas may have more lenient zoning regulations compared to urban or suburban zones. Consider the location's zoning designation and how it aligns with your off-grid plans.

Building Codes and Permits

Complying with building codes is essential to ensure the safety and legality of your off-grid dwelling.

- **Code Compliance:** Building codes are established to safeguard the health and safety of occupants. Familiarize yourself with local building codes to ensure that your off-grid structure meets the necessary safety standards.
- **Building Permits:** Obtain the required building permits before starting any construction. Failure to do so may result in legal consequences, and local authorities may require modifications or removal of unpermitted structures.
- **Alternative Building Methods:** Some areas have specific regulations regarding alternative building methods, such as earthbag construction or tiny homes. Research whether your chosen construction method complies with local codes.

Water Rights and Usage

Water is a critical resource for off-grid living, and understanding water rights is essential.

- **Water Rights Ownership:** In certain regions, water rights may be attached to the property. Research the ownership and usage rights associated with the water sources on your land to avoid legal conflicts.
- **Water Collection and Storage:** Ensure that your water collection and storage methods comply with local regulations. Some areas may have restrictions on rainwater harvesting or may require permits for certain water-related activities.

- **Well Drilling and Licensing:** If you plan to drill a well for water, investigate the licensing requirements. Well drilling regulations vary, and compliance is necessary to avoid legal issues.

Waste Management and Environmental Regulations

Proper waste management is not only an environmental responsibility but also subject to legal considerations.

- **Septic Systems:** If your off-grid property requires a septic system, adhere to regulations regarding installation and maintenance. Non-compliance can lead to environmental contamination and legal consequences.
- **Composting Toilets:** Some areas may have specific regulations regarding the use of composting toilets. Ensure that your waste disposal methods align with local environmental standards.

Energy Generation and Usage

Off-grid living often involves generating your own energy, and legal considerations apply to alternative energy systems.

- **Solar and Wind Regulations:** Check for any regulations related to the installation and operation of solar panels or wind turbines. Some areas may have restrictions on the size, location, or visual impact of these systems.
- **Grid Connection Policies:** Understand the policies regarding grid connection and net metering if you choose to have a hybrid off-grid system. Some regions have specific regulations governing the connection of off-grid properties to the utility grid.

Easements and Right-of-Way

Easements and right-of-way issues can impact your access to and use of your off-grid property.

- **Access Easements:** Ensure that you have legal access to your property. Access easements, which grant the right to use a specific route to reach your land, should be clearly defined and legally established.

- **Utility Easements:** Be aware of any utility easements that may exist on your property. These easements grant utility companies the right to access and maintain their infrastructure.

Community and Covenant Restrictions

Some off-grid properties may be subject to community restrictions or covenants.

- **Homeowners' Associations (HOAs):** If your property is part of an HOA, review the association's rules and restrictions. Some HOAs have specific guidelines that may impact off-grid practices.
- **Deed Restrictions:** Check for any deed restrictions on your property. Deed restrictions may limit certain activities or land uses, so understanding these restrictions is crucial.

Living off the grid requires a comprehensive understanding of the legal framework that governs land use, construction, resource management, and property rights. Researching and complying with local regulations will help ensure a lawful and sustainable off-grid lifestyle. As laws can vary significantly from one location to another, seeking legal advice and consulting local authorities is advisable to navigate the legal complexities of off-grid living successfully.

Chapter 2:

Establishing A Reliable Water Supply

Introduction: Foundations of Water Conservation and Sustainability

Water, the essence of life, is a finite resource that requires thoughtful management and preservation to ensure a sustainable future. As we face challenges such as climate change, population growth, and increasing demands on water sources, the need for water conservation and sustainability becomes paramount.

The Value of Water

Water is not merely a commodity; it is a precious and irreplaceable resource that sustains ecosystems, supports agriculture, and meets the basic needs of human life. Recognizing the inherent value of water is the first step towards building a foundation for conservation and sustainability.

Understanding Water Footprints

A crucial concept in water sustainability is the water footprint – the total amount of water used directly and indirectly in the production of goods and services. By comprehending the water footprint of products and activities, individuals and businesses can make informed choices to minimize their impact on water resources.

Efficient Water Use at Home

Residential water use constitutes a significant portion of overall consumption. Implementing efficient water practices at home is fundamental to conservation.

- **Water-Efficient Appliances:** The utilization of water-efficient appliances, including low-flow toilets and high-efficiency washing machines, can lower the amount of water that is consumed without affecting the capability of the device.
- **Smart Irrigation:** Implementing smart irrigation systems that consider weather conditions and plant water needs minimizes water waste in landscaping.
- **Fixing Leaks:** Addressing leaks promptly is crucial. Even small leaks can contribute to significant water loss over time.

Agricultural Water Management

Agriculture is a major consumer of water, and sustainable practices are essential for long-term food security.

- **Drip Irrigation and Precision Farming:** Precision irrigation methods, like drip systems, enhance water-use efficiency in agriculture by delivering water directly to the roots of plants.
- **Crop Selection:** Choosing crops that are well-suited to local climates and optimizing planting schedules contribute to water conservation in agriculture.
- **Soil Health:** Healthy soils retain water more effectively. Practices such as cover cropping and organic farming contribute to improved soil structure and water retention.

Building A Rainwater Harvesting System: Step by Step Project

A Rainwater Harvesting System is a vital no-grid survival project that efficiently collects and stores rainwater for various purposes. Using simple techniques, such as gutters and downspouts connected to storage tanks, it captures rain runoff from roofs. This harvested water can then be filtered and used for drinking, irrigation, or other essential needs. The system reduces dependency on traditional water sources, making it particularly valuable in off-grid scenarios or during emergencies. Implementing this project requires basic tools like gutters, pipes, and storage containers, making it accessible for DIY enthusiasts. Additionally, it promotes sustainability by conserving water resources and mitigating the impact of droughts.

Step 1: Assess Your Roof and Water Needs

Before starting the project, assess your roof area and estimate your water needs. The collection efficiency depends on the size and shape of your roof. Determine the purpose of collecting rainwater and the volume required to meet your needs.

Step 2: Gather Materials and Tools

Materials:

- **Gutters:** Collect rainwater from the roof.
- **Downspouts:** Direct water from gutters to the storage tank.
- **Leaf Guards:** Prevent debris from entering the system.
- **First Flush Diverter:** Diverts the initial dirty rainwater away from the tank.
- **Tank:** Storage for collected rainwater (choose a size based on your needs).
- **Tank Overflow System:** Redirect excess water when the tank is full.
- **Tank Screen:** Filters debris from entering the tank.
- **Pump (Optional):** For pressurized distribution.
- **Filters:** Additional filtration for potable water systems.
- **Piping:** Connects components.

Tools:

- Tape measure
- Hacksaw or pipe cutter
- Screwdriver
- Electric drill
- Pipe wrench
- Teflon tape
- Sealant

Step 3: Design the System

Design the rainwater harvesting system layout. Consider the slope of your roof, the placement of gutters, and the location of downspouts. Ensure the tank is positioned at a higher elevation than where the water is needed for gravitational flow.

Step 4: Install Gutters and Downspouts

- **Attach Gutters:** Install gutters along the edges of the roof. Use the tape measure to ensure a consistent slope towards the downspouts.
- **Install Downspouts:** Attach downspouts to direct water from the gutters to the storage tank.
- **Include Leaf Guards:** Install leaf guards at the top of each downspout to prevent debris from entering the system.

Step 5: First Flush Diverter Installation

- **Position Diverter:** Install the first flush diverter at the beginning of the downspout. This diverts the initial dirty rainwater away from the tank, improving water quality.
- **Connect Diverter:** Connect the diverter to the downspout using piping.

Step 6: Install Tank and Overflow System

- **Place the Tank:** Position the tank on a stable surface, considering the weight of the full tank.
- **Install Overflow System:** Attach the overflow system to redirect excess water away from the tank once it reaches capacity. This prevents overflows and potential damage.

Step 7: Install Tank Screen and Filter

- **Attach Screen:** Install a screen at the tank inlet to filter out debris. This prevents sediment buildup in the tank.

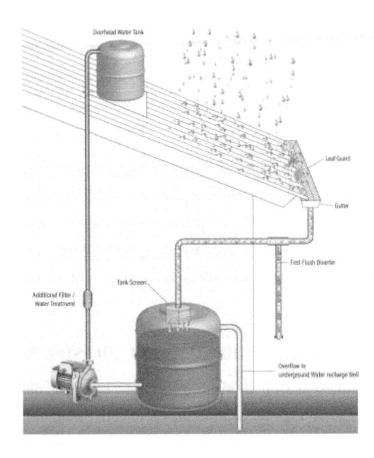

- **Install Additional Filters (Optional):** For systems that provide potable water, install additional filters to ensure water quality.

Step 8: Connect Piping and Optional Pump

- **Connect Piping:** Use piping to connect the various components, ensuring a sealed and secure fit.
- **Install Pump (Optional):** If pressurized water distribution is required, install a pump in the system. Connect it to the piping and ensure proper electrical connections.

Step 9: Test the System

Before relying on the system, test it to ensure proper functioning. Check for leaks, confirm that water is flowing correctly, and monitor the first flush diverter to see if it's effectively diverting dirty water.

Step 10: Maintenance and Monitoring

Regularly maintain and monitor the system. Clean gutters, remove debris from screens, and inspect the tank and components for any issues. This ensures the longevity and efficiency of the rainwater harvesting system.

Creating a rainwater harvesting system involves careful planning, proper installation, and regular maintenance. By following this step-by-step guide, you can harness the benefits of rainwater for various purposes while contributing to water conservation and sustainability. Adjustments may be necessary based on specific local regulations or additional considerations for potable water use. Always consult local authorities and professionals when in doubt.

Setting Up A Solar Water Distillation Unit: Step by Step Project

A Solar Water Distillation Unit is a no-grid survival project designed to produce clean drinking water using solar energy. This simple yet effective system harnesses the sun's power to evaporate water, leaving impurities behind and then condensing the vapor to collect purified water. The apparatus typically consists of a solar collector, a condensation surface, and a collection container. It requires minimal technology, relying on the sun's heat for the distillation process. This makes it a feasible option for off-grid living or emergency situations. The unit can be constructed using basic materials like glass or plastic, emphasizing its accessibility for DIY enthusiasts. By utilizing renewable energy, the Solar Water Distillation Unit offers a sustainable solution for obtaining safe drinking water without relying on external power sources.

Step 1: Gather Materials and Tools

Materials:

- **Sheet of Glass or Plastic:** Acts as the cover for the distillation unit.
- **Shallow Container:** For holding water to be distilled.
- **Heat-Resistant Container:** To collect distilled water.

- **Rubber Tubing:** For condensation collection.
- **Black Paint or Cloth:** To paint or cover the bottom of the shallow container.
- **Adhesive or Waterproof Sealant:** To seal joints.
- **Wood or Metal Frame:** To support the glass/plastic cover.
- **Reflective Material (Optional):** To enhance sunlight concentration.
- **Thermometer:** To measure temperature.
- **Basic Tools:** Screwdriver, saw, paintbrush, measuring tape.

Tools:

- Screwdriver
- Saw
- Paintbrush
- Measuring Tape

Step 2: Design and Layout

Design the solar water distillation unit layout. Consider the angle and orientation of the glass or plastic cover to maximize sunlight exposure. Ensure that the shallow container is positioned at an angle for water runoff.

Step 3: Prepare the Shallow Container

- **Paint or Cover:** Paint the bottom of the shallow container black or cover it with black cloth. This helps absorb solar radiation and increases the water temperature.
- **Position Container:** Place the shallow container on a frame, ensuring that it is at an angle for water to flow towards one end.

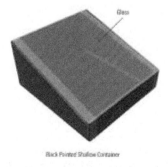

Black Painted Shallow Container

Step 4: Attach Condensation Collection Tube

- **Attach Tube:** Connect the rubber tubing to the low end of the shallow container to collect condensed water.
- **Position Collection Container:** Place the heat-resistant container at the other end of the tubing to collect distilled water.

Step 5: Construct the Frame

- **Build Frame:** Construct a frame using wood or metal to support the glass or plastic cover. The frame should hold the cover at an angle, allowing it to capture maximum sunlight.
- **Position Frame:** Position the frame over the shallow container, ensuring stability and proper alignment.

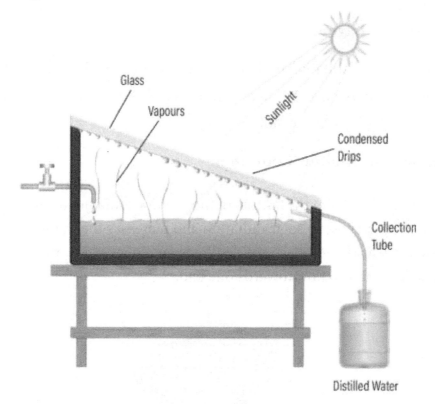

Step 6: Seal Joints and Gaps

- **Seal Joints:** Use adhesive or waterproof sealant to secure joints and prevent air leaks. This helps maintain a controlled environment inside the distillation unit.

20

- **Check Seals:** Ensure that all joints and gaps are sealed properly to prevent heat loss.

Step 7: Enhance Sunlight Concentration (Optional)

For increased efficiency, you may choose to enhance sunlight concentration by adding reflective material around the sides of the shallow container. This directs more sunlight towards the water surface.

Step 8: Test the System

- **Position in Sunlight:** Place the solar water distillation unit in direct sunlight. Position it so that the glass or plastic cover faces the sun.
- **Monitor Temperature:** Use a thermometer to monitor the temp. inside the unit. It should rise as the sunlight is absorbed.
- **Check Condensation:** Observe condensation forming on the glass or plastic cover and dripping down into the collection container.

Step 9: Collect Distilled Water

As the water inside the shallow container heats up, vapor rises, condenses on the cover, and then drips into the collection container as distilled water. Periodically check and collect the distilled water.

Step 10: Maintenance and Troubleshooting

Regularly check for any damage, leaks, or obstructions. Clean the glass or plastic cover to maintain optimal sunlight exposure. Troubleshoot any issues, such as inadequate temperature or condensation, and make necessary adjustments.

Building a solar water distillation unit is a rewarding and environmentally friendly way to produce clean drinking water. By harnessing solar energy, this DIY project provides a sustainable solution for water purification. Always consider local regulations and safety guidelines when working with materials and tools. This guide offers a basic framework, and adjustments can be made based on specific needs and conditions.

Creating A Gravity-Fed Water Filtration System: Step by Step Project

A Gravity-Fed Water Filtration System is a no-grid survival project that provides a reliable and low-tech method for purifying water. This system employs the force of gravity to move water through various filtration stages, removing impurities and contaminants. It typically consists of a series of filter elements, such as ceramic or activated carbon, housed in a container through which water flows. The gravitational pull facilitates the filtration process, making it suitable for off-grid scenarios where electricity is unavailable.

Step 1: Gather Materials and Tools

Materials:

- **Two Food-Grade Containers:** One for holding untreated water (source) and the other for filtered water.
- **Filter Media:** Activated carbon, ceramic, or any suitable water filter cartridge.
- **Drill with Bits:** For creating holes in containers.
- **Food-Grade Tubing:** For water transfer.
- **Spigot or Faucet Valve:** For controlled water dispensing.
- **Food-Grade Sealant or Silicone:** To seal drilled holes.
- **Filter Stand or Platform:** To elevate the top container.
- **Filter Mesh or Cloth (Optional):** For pre-filtration to remove larger particles.
- **Activated Carbon (Optional):** For enhanced filtration.
- **Basic Tools:** Screwdriver, utility knife, pliers, measuring tape.

Tools:

- Drill with Bits
- Screwdriver
- Utility Knife
- Pliers
- Measuring Tape

Step 2: Design and Layout

Design the gravity-fed water filtration system layout. Consider the placement of the filter media, tubing, and spigot. Ensure that the system is stable and that water can flow easily through the filtration process.

Step 3: Prepare the Top Container

- **Create Holes:** Use a drill to create holes near the bottom of the top container. The holes should accommodate the filter media and allow water to flow into the lower container.
- **Insert Filter Media:** Place the filter media (e.g., ceramic or activated carbon) into the container. Ensure a snug fit to prevent water from bypassing the filter.
- **Include Optional Pre-Filtration:** If using filter mesh or cloth for pre-filtration, secure it over the holes to capture larger particles before reaching the filter media.
- **Seal Holes:** Apply food-grade sealant or silicone around the holes to prevent leaks.

Step 4: Elevate the Top Container

- **Place Filter Stand:** Position the filter stand or platform at a suitable height to elevate the top container. This elevation helps create the necessary gravitational force for water flow.
- **Secure Top Container:** Place the top container on the filter stand, ensuring stability.

Step 5: Connect Tubing and Spigot

- **Insert Tubing:** Connect one end of the food-grade tubing to the bottom of the top container, extending into the space above the filter media.
- **Attach Spigot:** Connect the other end of the tubing to the spigot or faucet valve. Secure it tightly to prevent leaks.
- **Place Bottom Container:** Position the bottom container beneath the spigot to collect filtered water.

Step 6: Test for Leaks

Before using the system, conduct a leak test. Fill the top container with water, open the spigot, and check for any leaks around the drilled holes, tubing connections, or spigot.

Step 7: Optional Activated Carbon Layer (Enhanced Filtration)

If desired, include a layer of activated carbon above the filter media inside the top container. This can enhance the filtration process by adsorbing impurities from the water.

Step 8: Fill and Prime the System

- **Fill the Top Container:** Pour untreated water into the top container, ensuring it reaches the level above the filter media.
- **Prime the System:** Allow water to flow through the system until air bubbles are no longer visible. This primes the filter media and ensures effective filtration.

Step 9: Dispense Filtered Water

Open the spigot, and filtered water will flow from the top container into the bottom container. The gravitational force helps move the water through the filter media, effectively removing impurities.

Step 10: Maintenance and Cleaning

Regularly clean the filter media and tubing to maintain optimal performance. Replace the filter media as recommended by the manufacturer. Clean the containers and spigot to prevent bacterial growth.

Creating a gravity-fed water filtration system is a practical and cost-effective way to ensure access to clean water in various settings. This DIY project offers a straightforward design suitable for small-scale applications. Adjustments can be made based on specific needs and conditions. Always consider local regulations and safety guidelines when working with materials and tools.

Chapter 3:

Harnessing Renewable Energy

Introduction: An Overview of Alternative Energy Options

In the face of environmental challenges and a growing demand for energy, the exploration and adoption of alternative energy sources have become imperative. Conventional approaches to energy generation, which heavily depend on fossil fuels, contribute significantly to environmental deterioration and the exacerbation of climate change. As a response to these concerns, alternative energy options have gained prominence, offering sustainable and environmentally friendly alternatives.

Understanding the Need for Alternatives

The conventional energy landscape, dominated by fossil fuels, poses significant threats to the environment, including air and water pollution, habitat destruction, and the emission of greenhouse gases. The pressing necessity to make the switch to alternative energy sources is a direct result of the compelling need to reduce the effects of climate change, reduce reliance on finite resources, and establish a more sustainable energy infrastructure.

Solar Power: Harnessing the Energy of the Sun

Solar power stands out as one of the other forms of energy that is both plentiful and readily available with its abundance. Solar panels are able to turn sunlight into electricity because they are able to capture sunlight through the use of photovoltaic cells. This clean and renewable energy option has seen remarkable advancements, with solar farms and residential installations becoming more prevalent. Despite its immense potential, challenges such as intermittency and the need for energy storage solutions persist.

Wind Energy: Tapping into the Power of the Breeze

Wind power stands out as a notable alternative, utilizing the kinetic energy of the wind and transforming it into electricity via wind turbines. As technology improves, wind farms, both onshore and offshore, contribute significantly to the global energy mix. However, challenges include the intermittent nature of wind and potential environmental impacts, exceptionally in terms of wildlife and aesthetics.

Hydroelectric Power: Exploiting the Force of Flowing Water

Hydroelectric power involves capturing the energy of moving water. Dams and turbines play an important role in transforming the kinetic energy of water into electrical energy. While this source is reliable and can provide a consistent power supply, concerns over ecosystem disruption, sedimentation, and the displacement of communities in dam construction remain.

Geothermal Energy: Tapping into Earth's Internal Heat

Geothermal energy exploits the heat beneath the Earth's surface to produce steam, which is then used to generate electricity. This form of alternative energy is reliable and produces low emissions, making it a viable option. However, its applicability is geographically limited to regions with significant geothermal activity.

Biomass: Converting Organic Matter into Energy

Biomass involves the conversion of organic materials, such as wood, crop residues, and organic waste, into energy. This can be achieved through combustion, fermentation, or other biological processes. While biomass can be a renewable and carbon-neutral energy source, concerns about deforestation, land use, and emissions from combustion processes exist.

Tidal and Wave Energy: Harnessing the Power of the Oceans

Tidal and wave energy tap into the kinetic energy of ocean tides and waves to generate electricity. These sources have the advantage of predictability and high energy density.

However, the technology is still in its early stages, and challenges related to environmental impact,

At the same time, mankind is struggling to overcome the difficulties brought about by climate change and the limited nature of conventional sources of energy, the exploration and adoption of alternative energy options become not just a choice but a necessity. This overview provides a glimpse into the diverse landscape of alternative energy, each source offering unique advantages and facing distinct challenges. The future of energy lies in a comprehensive approach that combines various alternatives, integrates smart technologies, and prioritizes sustainability to pave the way for a cleaner and more resilient global energy infrastructure.

DIY Installation of Solar Panels: Step by Step Project

DIY Installation of Solar Panels is a no-grid survival project that empowers individuals to harness renewable energy for electricity needs. The process involves mounting photovoltaic panels on a suitable structure, typically a roof or ground-mounted frame. Basic tools, such as drills, screws, and wiring equipment, are essential for this project.

Start by determining the solar panel placement to maximize sunlight exposure. Connect the panels in series or parallel to achieve the desired voltage and current. Install an inverter to convert the generated DC power into AC power suitable for household use. Basic electrical knowledge is necessary for proper wiring and connection to the electrical system.

This DIY project offers energy independence, reducing reliance on traditional power sources. It's cost-effective and environmentally friendly, contributing to sustainable living. However, safety precautions and compliance with local regulations are crucial during installation.

Step 1: Determine Your Energy Needs and Site Suitability

- **Calculate Energy Needs:** The size of the solar system that you require can be determined by analyzing the amount of energy that you consume. This involves reviewing utility bills and understanding daily and monthly usage patterns.

- **Evaluate Site Suitability:** Ensure that your property receives adequate sunlight throughout the day. Check for shading from trees, buildings, or other obstructions that may impact solar panel efficiency.

Step 2: Gather Materials and Tools

Materials:

- **Solar Panels:** Choose high-quality solar panels with the appropriate wattage for your energy needs.
- **Mounting System:** Racking or mounting system to secure solar panels to the roof.
- **Inverter:** Converts DC electricity generated by the panels into AC electricity for home use.
- **Charge Controller (For Battery Systems):** Regulates the charge to batteries, if applicable.
- **Batteries (Optional):** For energy storage in off-grid systems.
- **Wiring and Connectors:** DC and AC wiring, connectors, and conduit.
- **Disconnect Switch:** Allows you to shut off the solar power system for maintenance or emergencies.
- **Grounding Equipment:** Grounding rods and cables for safety.
- **Roof Flashing and Sealant:** To secure panels to the roof without leaks.

Tools:

- Drill with Bits
- Wrenches
- Screwdriver
- Wire Strippers
- Multimeter
- Ladder
- Roof Anchor (For Roof Work)
- Safety Gear: Gloves, safety glasses, and a hard hat.

Step 3: Create a Solar Panel Layout Plan

- **Roof Assessment:** Evaluate the roof structure and identify the best location for solar panel placement. Consider the tilt and orientation for optimal sunlight exposure.
- **Panel Layout:** Create a layout plan that maximizes available roof space and minimizes shading. Ensure panels are evenly spaced and securely mounted.

Step 4: Install Mounting System

- **Locate Roof Rafters:** Use a stud finder to locate roof rafters. Mounting brackets should be secured to these structural elements.
- **Attach Mounting Brackets:** Install mounting brackets or rails on the roof according to the layout plan. Use roof flashing and sealant to prevent leaks.
- **Secure Solar Panels:** Attach solar panels to the mounting brackets or rails, securing them with bolts and washers. Follow the manufacturer's guidelines for proper installation.

Step 5: Connect Solar Panels in Series or Parallel

- **Determine Wiring Configuration:** Decide whether to connect solar panels in series or parallel based on your system voltage and design preferences.
- **Connect Solar Panels:** Use DC wiring and connectors to link the solar panels. Follow the wiring diagram provided by the panel manufacturer.
- **Install Junction Boxes (Optional):** Install junction boxes to protect wiring connections and facilitate future maintenance.

Step 6: Install Inverter and Charge Controller

- **Mount Inverter:** Install the inverter in a well-ventilated and easily accessible location. Link the inverter to the primary electrical panel.
- **Connect Charge Controller (If Applicable):** If using batteries for energy storage, connect the charge controller to regulate charging and discharging.
- **Connect Wiring:** Use proper wiring to connect the solar panels to the inverter and charge controller. Follow the manufacturer's guidelines for wire sizing and connections.

Step 7: Install Disconnect Switch and Grounding

- **Install Disconnect Switch:** Place a disconnect switch between the solar panels and the inverter. This switch allows you to shut off the solar power system for maintenance or emergencies.
- **Ground the System:** Install grounding equipment, including grounding rods and cables. Ensure proper grounding to enhance system safety.

Step 8: Test and Commission the System

- **Check Wiring Connections:** Verify all wiring connections to ensure they are secure and properly connected.
- **Test Voltage:** Use a multimeter to measure DC voltage at various points in the system. Ensure that the voltage matches the specifications of the solar panels and inverter.
- **Commission the System:** Turn on the solar power system and monitor its performance. Check the inverter display for proper functioning.

Step 9: Optional Battery Connection (For Off-Grid Systems)

- **Install Batteries:** If your system includes energy storage, install the batteries in a well-ventilated and secure location.
- **Connect Batteries:** Use appropriate wiring to connect the batteries to the charge controller and inverter. Follow the manufacturer's guidelines for battery connections.

Step 10: Monitor and Maintain the System

- **Monitor Performance:** Regularly monitor the performance of your solar power system. Many inverters come with monitoring capabilities that allow you to track energy production.
- **Perform Maintenance:** Inspect the system for dirt, debris, or shading that may affect performance. Clean the solar panels as needed and trim any overhanging branches that could cause shading.

Installing solar panels as a DIY project requires careful planning, attention to safety, and compliance with local regulations.

Constructing A Small Wind Turbine for Energy: Step by Step Project

A small wind turbine is a no-grid survival project designed to harness wind energy for off-grid power generation. Compact and efficient, these turbines typically feature a rotor and blades that capture wind energy, converting it into electricity for essential needs. These projects are well-suited for remote locations or emergency situations where traditional power sources are unavailable. The simplicity of small wind turbines allows for easy installation and maintenance, making them accessible for DIY enthusiasts and off-grid communities. Their scalability makes them adaptable to varying energy demands, providing a sustainable solution for powering essential appliances and devices. While weather-dependent, these turbines can contribute to a reliable and eco-friendly energy source, promoting self-sufficiency and resilience in off-grid scenarios.

Step 1: Gather Materials and Tools

Materials:

- **Generator:** DC motor or permanent magnet alternator.
- **Blades:** Lightweight and aerodynamic material such as PVC, wood, or fiberglass.
- **Hub:** Connects the blades to the generator.
- **Tower:** Sturdy pipe or tubing for mounting the turbine.
- **Tail:** Helps the turbine face into the wind.
- **Charge Controller:** Regulates the power output and prevents overcharging.
- **Battery (Optional):** For energy storage in off-grid systems.
- **Inverter (Optional):** Converts DC power to AC for home use.
- **Wiring and Connectors:** Suitable wires for connecting components.
- **Base Plate and Anchors:** For stabilizing the tower.
- **Diodes:** Prevents the battery from discharging through the turbine.
- **Guy Wires and Anchors:** For tower stability.

Tools:

- Drill with Bits
- Saw
- Screwdriver
- Wrenches
- Pliers
- Multimeter
- Soldering Iron
- Measuring Tape
- Safety Gear: Gloves, safety glasses, and a hard hat.

Step 2: Design the Wind Turbine

- **Determine Blade Length:** Calculate the optimal blade length based on the diameter of the turbine. Longer blades capture more wind energy.
- **Choose Blade Design:** Select a blade design that is aerodynamic and easy to manufacture. Common designs include flat blades or twisted blades.
- **Design the Hub:** Create a hub that securely connects the blades to the generator. It should be lightweight and able to withstand wind forces.

Step 3: Construct Blades and Hub

- **Cut Blade Material:** Cut the chosen blade material into the desired length and shape. Ensure that all blades are identical for balance.
- **Attach Blades to the Hub:** Securely attach the blades to the hub using screws, bolts, or other suitable fasteners. Balance the blades to ensure smooth rotation.
- **Reinforce Hub:** Strengthen the hub to withstand wind forces. Reinforce with additional material or support structures if necessary.

Step 4: Assemble the Generator and Tail

- **Modify the Generator:** If using a DC motor, remove unnecessary components and attach the hub directly to the motor shaft. If using a permanent magnet alternator, connect it to the hub.

- **Install the Tail:** Attach the tail to the back of the turbine to help it face into the wind. The tail can be a simple vane or fin that guides the turbine.

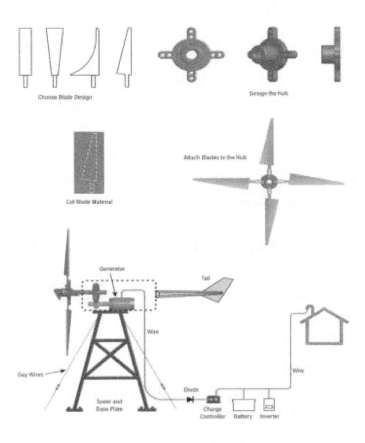

Step 5: Construct the Tower and Base Plate

- **Cut Tower Material:** Cut the tower material to the desired height, considering local wind patterns and clearance requirements. Ensure that the tower is sturdy and able to support the turbine.
- **Attach Base Plate:** Secure the tower to a base plate using anchors. The base plate should be heavy and wide enough to stabilize the tower.

Step 6: Install Guy Wires (for Tall Towers)

- **Determine Guy Wire Placement:** If the tower is tall, install guy wires to provide additional stability. Determine the optimal placement and angles for the guy wires.

- **Anchor Guy Wires:** Secure the guy wires to anchors in the ground. Tension the wires appropriately to support the tower.

Step 7: Install Charge Controller, Battery, and Inverter

- **Mount the Charge Controller:** Install the charge controller near the base of the tower to regulate the power output from the generator.
- **Connect Battery (Optional):** If using a battery for energy storage, connect it to the charge controller. Use appropriate wiring and connectors.
- **Install Inverter (Optional):** If converting DC power to AC for home use, install the inverter. Connect it to the battery and the electrical system.

Step 8: Wiring and Electrical Connections

- **Connect Generator to Charge Controller:** Use appropriate wiring to connect the generator to the charge controller.
- **Connect Charge Controller to Battery:** Connect the charge controller to the battery using suitable wires and connectors.
- **Connect Battery to Inverter (Optional):** If using an inverter, connect it to the battery to convert DC power to AC.
- **Install Diodes:** Install diodes to prevent the battery from discharging through the turbine when it's not generating power.

Step 9: Test the Wind Turbine System

- **Check Electrical Connections:** Verify all electrical connections for accuracy and secureness.
- **Measure Voltage Output:** Use a multimeter to measure the voltage output from the generator while manually turning the blades.
- **Monitor Battery Charging (Optional):** If using a battery, monitor its charging status as the wind turbine generates power.

Step 10: Maintenance and Monitoring

- **Regular Inspections:** Periodically inspect the turbine, blades, tower, and electrical components for signs of wear, damage, or corrosion.

- **Adjust Blade Angle (Optional):** If possible, adjust the blade angle to optimize performance based on wind conditions.
- **Monitor Energy Production:** Keep track of the energy production to assess the effectiveness of the wind turbine.

Building a small wind turbine can provide a sense of accomplishment and contribute to sustainable energy generation. It's crucial to follow safety guidelines, consult local regulations, and consider professional advice when needed. Additionally, this guide offers a basic framework, and adjustments may be necessary based on specific conditions and requirements. By harnessing wind power through a DIY wind turbine, you may make a contribution to a future energy system that is cleaner and more sustainable.

Setting Up A Micro-Hydroelectric Power System: Step by Step Project

A micro-hydroelectric power system is a no-grid survival project that harnesses the energy from flowing water to generate electricity for off-grid locations. Typically designed for small-scale applications, these systems utilize the kinetic energy of rivers or streams to turn turbines, converting water power into electrical energy. The compact nature of micro-hydro systems makes them suitable for remote areas, providing a sustainable and reliable energy source. These projects often involve the installation of water turbines, penstocks, and generators, requiring careful consideration of water flow and site characteristics. Micro-hydro systems contribute to self-sufficiency by offering a continuous and renewable power supply, even in off-grid settings.

Step 1: Assess the Hydroelectric Potential

- **Evaluate Water Source:** Identify a reliable water source with a consistent flow. The greater the flow, the more power the system can generate.
- **Determine Head and Flow:** Measure the vertical drop (head) and the flow rate of the water. These factors determine the potential power output of the micro-hydro system.

Step 2: Gather Materials and Tools

Materials:

- **Water Turbine:** Choose a suitable water turbine based on head and flow characteristics.
- **Generator:** AC or DC generator compatible with the selected turbine.
- **Piping and Penstock:** Pipes to channel water from the source to the turbine.
- **Charge Controller:** Regulates the electrical output to prevent overcharging.
- **Battery (Optional):** For storing generated energy in off-grid systems.
- **Inverter (Optional):** Converts DC power to AC for home use.
- **Wiring and Connectors:** Suitable wires and connectors for electrical connections.
- **Support Structures:** Concrete or metal structures to support the turbine and generator.
- **Anchors and Fasteners:** Bolts, nuts, and anchors for securing components.
- **Valves and Gates:** Control the flow of water through the system.
- **Electrical Panel:** To centralize electrical connections.

Tools:

- Drill with Bits
- Saw
- Wrenches
- Pliers
- Multimeter
- Level
- Measuring Tape
- Safety Gear: Gloves, safety glasses, and a hard hat.

Step 3: Design the Micro-Hydro System

- **Select Turbine Type:** Choose a water turbine based on the head and flow characteristics. Common types include Pelton, Turgo, and Crossflow turbines.
- **Design Penstock:** Determine the size and route of the penstock (pipe that carries water to the turbine). Account for friction losses and select materials accordingly.
- **Position Components:** Plan the location of the turbine, generator, and support structures. Ensure proper alignment for efficient power generation.

Step 4: Construct Support Structures and Penstock

- **Build Support Structures:** Construct concrete or metal structures to support the turbine and generator. Ensure stability and alignment.
- **Assemble Penstock:** Install the penstock, ensuring a gradual downward slope toward the turbine. Use appropriate anchors and supports to secure the penstock.

Step 5: Install Turbine and Generator

- **Position Turbine:** Install the water turbine in the designated location. Ensure that it aligns with the flow of water and has the proper clearance.
- **Connect Turbine to Generator:** Attach the turbine to the generator using a coupling or appropriate connection method. Securely fasten and align the components.
- **Secure Generator:** Mount the generator in a secure and weather-resistant location. Connect it to the turbine with appropriate wiring.
-

Step 6: Install Valves and Gates

- **Install Valves:** Place valves in the penstock to control the flow of water. This allows you to regulate the power output of the system.
- **Include Gates (Optional):** Consider adding gates for additional control over water flow. This can be particularly useful for maintenance or during periods of low energy demand.

Step 7: Connect Electrical Components

- **Connect Generator to Charge Controller:** Use appropriate wiring to connect the generator to the charge controller. This regulates the electrical output and prevents overcharging.
- **Connect Charge Controller to Battery (Optional):** If using a battery for energy storage, connect the charge controller to the battery with suitable wiring and connectors.
- **Connect Battery to Inverter (Optional):** If converting DC power to AC for home use, connect the battery to the inverter using proper wiring.

- **Install Electrical Panel:** Centralize electrical connections in an electrical panel. Label circuits for clarity.

Step 8: Test the Micro-Hydro System

- **Open Valves:** Gradually open the valves to allow water to flow through the system. Monitor the turbine and generator for proper functioning.
- **Check Electrical Output:** Measure the electrical output using a multimeter. Ensure that the charge controller is regulating the output correctly.
- **Monitor Battery Charging (Optional):** If using a battery, monitor its charging status as the micro-hydro system generates power.

Step 9: Optional Battery Connection (For Off-Grid Systems)

- **Install Batteries:** If energy storage is desired, install batteries in a suitable location. Ensure proper ventilation and security.
- **Connect Batteries:** Use appropriate wiring to connect the batteries to the charge controller and inverter. Follow the manufacturer's guidelines for battery connections.

Step 10: Maintenance and Monitoring

- **Regular Inspections:** Periodically inspect the turbine, generator, penstock, and electrical components for signs of wear, damage, or corrosion.
- **Adjust Valves and Gates:** Adjust valves and gates as needed to optimize energy production based on water flow conditions.
- **Monitor Energy Production:** Keep track of energy production to assess the effectiveness of the micro-hydro system.

Setting up a micro-hydroelectric power system provides a reliable and renewable energy source. It's crucial to follow safety guidelines, consult local regulations, and seek professional advice when needed. Additionally, this guide offers a basic framework, and adjustments may be necessary based on specific conditions and requirements. By harnessing water power through a DIY micro-hydro system, you may make a contribution to a future energy system that is cleaner and more sustainable.

Chapter 4:

Insulation and Energy Efficiency

Techniques

Introduction: Sustainable Heating and Cooling Systems

In the quest for a more sustainable and environmentally friendly future, the focus on sustainable heating and cooling systems has become increasingly vital. During a time when the international community is struggling to cope with the obstacles that climate change presents and the imperative to cut emissions of greenhouse gases, the way we heat and cool our homes and buildings plays a pivotal role in mitigating environmental impact. This introduction explores the significance of adopting sustainable heating and cooling technologies, delving into the principles, benefits, and advancements that define the transition towards eco-friendly solutions.

Understanding the Need for Sustainability

Traditional heating and cooling methods often rely on fossil fuels, contributing significantly to carbon emissions and environmental degradation. The imperative to transition towards sustainable alternatives arises from the need to curb climate change, minimize reliance on finite resources, and create more resilient and energy-efficient systems.

Principles of Sustainable Heating and Cooling

Sustainable heating and cooling systems are characterized by their reliance on renewable energy sources, high energy efficiency, and minimal environmental impact. These systems aim to harness natural elements such as sunlight, air, and geothermal heat, employing advanced technologies to optimize energy use and reduce carbon footprints.

Solar Heating

Solar heating stands out as a prominent sustainable solution, utilizing the abundant energy from the sun to provide warmth. Solar thermal collectors seize sunlight and transform it into thermal energy, suitable for either space heating or generating hot water for residential and commercial applications. The simplicity and effectiveness of solar heating contribute to its widespread adoption as a sustainable heating method.

Geothermal Systems

Geothermal heating and cooling systems leverage the constant temperature beneath the Earth's surface. By circulating fluid through underground loops, these systems extract heat for warming in winter and dissipate excess heat for cooling in summer. Geothermal systems are known for their high efficiency and reliability, offering a year-round sustainable solution.

Air-Source and Ground-Source Heat Pumps

Heat pumps exhibit versatility by efficiently offering both heating and cooling functions through the transfer of heat between the air or ground and the interior of a structure. Extracting heat from the outdoor air characterizes **air-source heat pumps**, whereas **ground-source heat pumps** leverage the consistently stable temperature of the ground. These systems are energy-efficient and can significantly reduce reliance on traditional heating and cooling methods.

Biomass Heating

Biomass heating utilizes organic materials, such as wood pellets or agricultural residues, as a renewable energy source. Biomass boilers and stoves burn these materials, releasing heat for space heating. When managed sustainably, biomass heating can be a carbon-neutral option, as the carbon released during combustion is offset by the carbon absorbed by the plants during their growth.

Challenges and Advancements

While the adoption of sustainable heating and cooling systems is growing, challenges persist. Affordability, accessibility, and public awareness are factors that influence the widespread implementation of these technologies. However, ongoing advancements in materials, design, and policy support are driving innovation and making sustainable systems more accessible to a broader audience.

Benefits of Sustainable Systems

The benefits of transitioning to sustainable heating and cooling are manifold. Reduced environmental impact, lower energy costs, and increased energy independence are among the advantages. Additionally, sustainable systems contribute to improved air quality, reduced reliance on non-renewable resources, and enhanced resilience to the impacts of climate change.

Embracing sustainable heating and cooling systems is not just a technological choice; it's a commitment to a greener, more resilient future. As we navigate the complexities of climate change and environmental stewardship, the shift towards these eco-friendly solutions becomes imperative.

Solar Water Heater Installation: Step by Step Project

A solar water heater is a crucial component in off-grid survival projects. This simple yet effective technology harnesses sunlight to heat water, providing a sustainable and energy-efficient solution. Consisting of solar collectors and a storage tank, the system absorbs sunlight, converting it into thermal energy to warm the water. This setup requires minimal maintenance, making it ideal for remote locations where conventional power sources are scarce. It ensures a reliable supply of hot water for cooking, cleaning, and personal hygiene, promoting self-sufficiency in off-grid environments. Additionally, solar water heaters reduce dependence on non-renewable energy sources, mitigating environmental impact. In survival scenarios, this technology enhances resilience by offering a dependable source of warm water for essential needs, contributing to a more sustainable and self-reliant off-grid lifestyle.

Step 1: Gather Materials and Tools

Materials:

- **Solar Collector Panels:** Flat-plate or evacuated tube collectors to absorb sunlight.
- **Solar Storage Tank:** Insulated tank to store heated water.
- **Pump:** Circulates water between the collector and the tank.
- **Controller:** Regulates the system by activating the pump when sunlight is available.
- **Heat Exchanger (Optional):** Transfers heat to the water in the tank.
- **Check Valve:** Prevents backflow in the system.
- **Pressure Relief Valve:** Releases excess pressure.
- **Expansion Tank:** Accommodates changes in water volume due to temperature fluctuations.
- **Piping and Connectors:** For water circulation.
- **Insulation:** Ensures minimal heat loss from pipes.
- **Frame or Mounting Structure:** Supports and positions the collector panels.
- **Fasteners and Anchors:** Secure components in place.

Tools:

- Drill with Bits
- Wrenches
- Screwdriver
- Pipe Cutter
- Multimeter
- Tape Measure
- Roof Anchor (For Roof Work)
- Safety Gear: Gloves, safety glasses, and a hard hat.

Step 2: Choose the Location and Orientation

- **Select a Sunny Location:** Choose a spot with maximum sunlight exposure throughout the day.
- **Consider Roof Angle:** Position the solar collector panels at an angle matching the latitude of your location for optimal sunlight absorption.

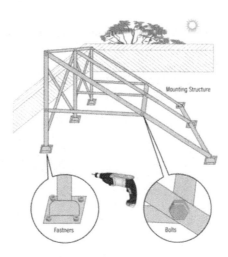

Step 3: Install the Mounting Structure

- **Attach Mounts to Roof:** Securely attach the mounting structure to the roof using anchors and fasteners. Ensure a stable and level foundation.
- **Position the Collector Panels:** Install the solar collector panels on the mounting structure, ensuring they face the sun at the correct angle.

Step 4: Connect the Collector Panels to the Storage Tank

- **Install Piping:** Connect piping from the collector panels to the solar storage tank. Use appropriate connectors and insulation to minimize heat loss.
- **Install Check Valve:** Place a check valve in the piping to prevent backflow when the pump is not in operation.

Step 5: Install the Pump and Controller

- **Position the Pump:** Install the pump in the piping system, ensuring it can circulate water between the collector panels and the storage tank.
- **Connect the Controller:** Install the controller to regulate the pump's operation based on sunlight availability. Connect the controller to the pump and power source.

Step 6: Install the Solar Storage Tank

- **Position the Tank:** Place the solar storage tank in a convenient location, preferably close to the collector panels to minimize piping length.
- **Connect the Tank to the Collector Panels:** Connect the piping from the collector panels to the solar storage tank. Ensure tight and secure connections.

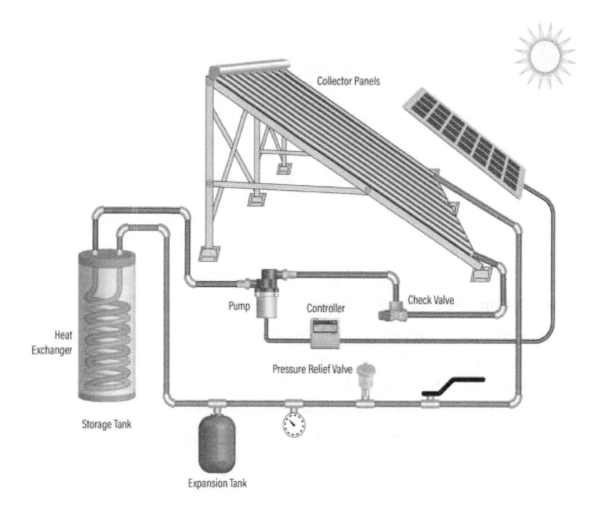

Step 7: Install Heat Exchanger and Additional Components (Optional)

- **Install Heat Exchanger:** If using a heat exchanger, connect it to the solar storage tank and the existing water heater system.
- **Connect Pressure Relief Valve:** Install a pressure relief valve to release excess pressure in the system.
- **Install Expansion Tank:** Connect the expansion tank to accommodate changes in water volume due to temperature fluctuations.

Step 8: Test the System

- **Check Connections:** Verify all connections are tight and secure.
- **Turn on the System:** Activate the pump and controller. Monitor water circulation and check for any leaks or issues.

Step 9: Monitor and Adjust Settings

- **Monitor Performance:** Keep track of water temperature and system performance.
- **Adjust Controller Settings:** Fine-tune the controller settings based on seasonal variations to optimize energy capture.

Step 10: Regular Maintenance

- **Inspect Components:** Regularly check the collector panels, piping, and other elements for any indications of wear, harm, or corrosion.
- **Clean Collector Panels:** Keep the collector panels clean from dirt or debris to maximize sunlight absorption.

Setting up a solar water heater offers a pragmatic approach to tap into renewable energy sources and diminish dependence on conventional heating techniques. This guide offers a basic framework, but it's crucial to consider specific conditions and consult with professionals when needed. By implementing a solar water heating system, you contribute to a more sustainable and energy-efficient future while enjoying the benefits of cost-effective and eco-friendly hot water.

Building A Wood Stove or Rocket Stove: Step by Step Project

A wood stove or rocket stove is a remarkable heating appliance that offers both efficiency and eco-friendliness in heating spaces. It utilizes wood or biomass as fuel, making it a sustainable and renewable energy option. These stoves are designed to maximize the combustion process, resulting in a more efficient use of fuel and reduced emissions.

One of the major advantages of wood and rocket stoves is their eco-friendliness. Wood is a renewable resource, and when burned in a well-designed stove, the emissions are significantly reduced compared to traditional open fires or older, inefficient stoves. Moreover, the use of biomass as fuel contributes to a closed carbon cycle, as the carbon dioxide released during combustion is absorbed by growing trees, creating a sustainable energy loop.

Step 1: Gather Materials and Tools

Materials:

- **Steel or Metal Sheet:** For constructing the stove body.
- **Insulation Material:** Vermiculite or ceramic fiber for insulating the combustion chamber.
- **Metal Pipe:** For the chimney or exhaust.
- **Fire Bricks or Refractory Cement (Optional):** For the combustion chamber lining.
- **Grate or Grid:** To support the fuel.
- **Metal Grate or Expanded Metal:** For the cooking surface.
- **Door Hinge and Latch:** For the stove door.
- **High-Temperature Paint:** To protect and finish the stove.
- **High-Temperature Sealant:** For sealing joints and connections.

Tools:

- Angle Grinder with Cutting Discs
- Welder or Rivets
- Drill with Bits
- Screwdriver
- Tape Measure
- Level
- Safety Gear: Welding mask, gloves, safety glasses, and a welding jacket.

Step 2: Design the Stove

- **Decide on Size and Dimensions:** Determine the size of the stove based on your heating or cooking needs.
- **Sketch the Design:** Plan the layout, considering the combustion chamber, air intake, and chimney placement.

Step 3: Cut and Shape the Metal Sheet

- **Cut the Metal Sheet:** Use an angle grinder to cut the metal sheet according to your design.

- **Shape the Parts:** Cut and shape the metal pieces for the combustion chamber, air intake, and chimney.

Step 4: Assemble the Combustion Chamber

- **Weld or Rivet the Parts:** Assemble the combustion chamber by welding or riveting the cut metal pieces together.
- **Attach the Grate or Grid:** Weld or attach the grate to support the fuel.

Step 5: Include Insulation and Combustion Chamber Lining (Optional)

- **Place Insulation Material:** Line the combustion chamber with vermiculite or ceramic fiber for insulation.
- **Use Fire Bricks or Refractory Cement (Optional):** Optionally, include fire bricks or apply refractory cement to the combustion chamber for improved durability.

Step 6: Create the Air Intake System

- **Cut Air Intake Holes:** Cut holes in the stove body to create an air intake system.
- **Include Adjustable Damper (Optional):** Install a damper to control the airflow and adjust the combustion intensity.

Step 7: Construct the Chimney or Exhaust System

- **Attach the Metal Pipe:** Weld or attach the metal pipe to the top of the combustion chamber to serve as the chimney or exhaust.
- **Extend the Pipe:** Extend the metal pipe to the desired height, ensuring it vents safely outdoors.

Step 8: Install the Cooking Surface (Optional)

- **Include a Metal Grate or Expanded Metal:** Weld or attach a metal grate or expanded metal above the combustion chamber to serve as the cooking surface.
- **Ensure Stability:** Ensure the cooking surface is stable and securely attached.

Step 9: Install the Door

- **Cut a Door Opening:** Cut an opening for the door on the stove body.

- **Attach the Hinge and Latch:** Weld or attach the door hinge and latch to secure the door.

Step 10: Paint and Finish the Stove

- **Apply High-Temperature Paint:** Paint the entire stove with high-temperature paint to protect it from corrosion.
- **Seal Joints with High-Temperature Sealant:** Apply high-temperature sealant to joints and connections for airtightness.

Step 11: Test and Use the Stove

- **Perform a Test Burn:** Place a small amount of fuel in the combustion chamber and perform a test burn to ensure proper airflow and combustion.
- **Adjust Airflow:** If necessary, adjust the air intake and damper to achieve optimal combustion.

Step 12: Regular Maintenance

- **Inspect and Clean:** Periodically inspect the stove for wear, damage, or corrosion. Clean out ash and debris from the combustion chamber.
- **Reapply Paint as Needed:** Reapply high-temperature paint as needed to maintain the stove's appearance and protection.

Building a wood stove or rocket stove is a satisfying and practical project that provides an efficient and sustainable heating or cooking solution. This guide offers a basic framework, but it's crucial to adapt the design based on specific needs and conditions. By constructing your own stove, you contribute to a more sustainable and self-sufficient lifestyle while enjoying the benefits of renewable energy.

Description Passive Cooling Techniques

Passive cooling employs natural elements and principles in its design strategy to sustain or reduce indoor temperatures without dependence on mechanical systems. This sustainable approach is particularly beneficial in reducing energy consumption, creating comfortable living spaces, and mitigating the urban heat island effect.

1. **Natural Ventilation**

Natural ventilation involves designing spaces to facilitate the movement of air without the need for mechanical systems. This is achieved through the strategic placement of windows, doors, and vents to allow for cross-ventilation.

Homes, offices, and buildings in moderate climates can benefit from natural ventilation. Incorporating operable windows and designing building orientations to capture prevailing winds enhances the effectiveness of this technique.

2. **Thermal Mass**

Thermal mass pertains to substances capable of absorbing, retaining, and subsequently releasing heat. By incorporating these materials into a building's structure, they can stabilize indoor temperatures by absorbing excess heat during the day and releasing it at night.

Homes or commercial structures can benefit from the use of stone, concrete, or adobe as construction materials to leverage thermal mass. This method proves especially impactful in dry climates characterized by substantial temperature variations between day and night.

3. **Cool Roofs**

Cool roofs are crafted to deflect a greater amount of sunlight while minimizing heat absorption in contrast to conventional roofing systems. This diminishes the transfer of heat into the structure, thereby sustaining cooler indoor temperatures.

Cool roofs are suitable for both residential and commercial buildings. They are particularly effective in warmer climates, helping to reduce cooling energy consumption and improve overall comfort.

4. **Shading**

Shading involves the strategic placement of elements such as awnings, overhangs, or vegetation to block or filter sunlight. This prevents direct sunlight from entering a space, reducing solar heat gain.

Shading is versatile and can be applied to residential homes, commercial buildings, and outdoor spaces. Deciduous trees and adjustable shading devices are effective in providing shade during the hot months while allowing sunlight during the cooler seasons.

5. Earth Sheltering

Earth sheltering involves using the thermal mass of the earth to maintain a more stable indoor temperature. Buildings are partially or entirely surrounded by soil, providing insulation and reducing temperature fluctuations.

Earth sheltering is well-suited for homes in colder climates or areas prone to extreme temperature variations. It's also employed in commercial buildings and can be integrated into hillside or underground construction.

6. Cross-Ventilation and Stack Effect

Cross-ventilation relies on wind pressure differences to move air through a building. The stack effect utilizes the principle that warm air rises, creating a natural upward airflow. Both techniques promote air circulation and heat dissipation.

Residential buildings, especially those with open floor plans, can benefit from cross-ventilation. The stack effect is effective in taller buildings, with openings strategically placed to allow warm air to rise and escape.

7. Reflective Surfaces

Using reflective surfaces, such as light-colored paints or materials with high albedo, helps bounce sunlight away from buildings. This reduces the absorption of solar radiation and lowers indoor temperatures.

Reflective surfaces are beneficial in various settings, including residential homes, commercial buildings, and urban environments. They are particularly effective in regions with intense sunlight.

8. Night Ventilation

Night ventilation takes advantage of cooler nighttime temperatures to naturally cool indoor spaces. Windows are opened during the night to allow cool air to circulate and flush out heat accumulated during the day.

Residential homes and buildings in regions with significant diurnal temperature variations benefit from night ventilation. This technique is effective in promoting thermal comfort without the need for mechanical cooling systems.

9. **Cool Courtyards and Green Roofs**

Cool courtyards create shaded, open spaces within a building that promote natural airflow. Green roofs use vegetation to provide insulation and reduce heat absorption, contributing to a cooler environment.

Cool courtyards are common in residential architecture, enhancing outdoor living spaces. Green roofs are applied to a variety of structures, including homes, commercial buildings, and urban developments, contributing to energy efficiency and environmental sustainability.

10. **Insulation**

Proper insulation minimizes heat transfer between indoor and outdoor environments, helping to maintain a consistent indoor temperature.

Insulation is a fundamental passive cooling technique applied to walls, roofs, and floors in both residential and commercial buildings. It is essential in regions with extreme temperatures, preventing excessive heat gain or loss.

Passive cooling techniques offer sustainable solutions for maintaining comfortable indoor environments while reducing reliance on energy-intensive cooling systems. The effectiveness of these techniques depends on factors such as climate, building design, and local conditions. By integrating these methods into architectural practices, we can contribute to more energy-efficient and resilient built environments, fostering a sustainable and comfortable future.

Chapter 5:

Efficient Waste Management

Introduction: Initiating Effective Strategies for Waste Control

In a world where the impact of human activities on the environment is a growing concern, the management and control of waste have become pivotal for sustainable living. The way we generate, handle, and dispose of waste significantly influences the health of ecosystems, biodiversity, and the overall well-being of our planet. This introduction sets the stage for understanding the importance of waste control and explores effective strategies that individuals, communities, and industries can initiate to address this global challenge.

Understanding the Urgency

Waste, in its various forms, poses a multifaceted challenge that extends beyond overflowing landfills. Improper waste management leads to environmental repercussions such as pollution, the degradation of habitats, and the discharge of hazardous substances into the air, water, and soil. As our population grows and consumption patterns evolve, the volume of waste generated continues to escalate, requiring urgent and comprehensive solutions.

The Impact on Ecosystems and Human Health

Uncontrolled waste disposal has far-reaching consequences on ecosystems. Plastic pollution in oceans, for instance, threatens marine life, disrupts food chains, and contaminates seafood consumed by humans. Landfills emit greenhouse gases, contributing to climate change. Harmful chemicals from improperly managed waste sites can leach into groundwater, jeopardizing both environmental and human health. Recognizing these impacts is crucial in motivating collective efforts toward waste control.

Shifting Toward a Circular Economy

An effective waste control strategy involves transitioning from a linear economy, where products are used and discarded, to a circular economy. In a circular model, resources are reused, recycled, and repurposed, minimizing the need for continuous extraction and reducing the burden on waste management systems. Embracing this circular approach is fundamental in breaking the cycle of wasteful consumption and disposal.

Reducing Single-Use Plastics

Single-use plastics have become symbolic of our throwaway culture, contributing significantly to pollution. Initiatives aimed at reducing the production and consumption of single-use plastics, such as bans on plastic bags and the promotion of reusable alternatives, are essential steps in waste control. Encouraging businesses to adopt sustainable packaging practices further contributes to this shift.

Enhancing Waste Segregation and Recycling

Efficient waste segregation at the source is a cornerstone of effective recycling. Communities and industries should invest in infrastructure and systems that facilitate the separation of recyclables from general waste. Recycling not only conserves resources but also reduces the amount of waste destined for landfills, alleviating the environmental burden.

Investing in Waste-to-Energy Technologies

Waste-to-energy technologies provide an innovative solution by converting waste materials into energy. Processes such as incineration and anaerobic digestion can generate electricity or heat while minimizing the volume of waste. While careful consideration of environmental impacts is necessary, these technologies offer a viable option for reducing the reliance on fossil fuels and managing waste more sustainably.

Building A Home Composting System: Step by Step Project

A Home Composting System is a sustainable grid survival project that addresses waste management and promotes self-sufficiency. By composting kitchen scraps and organic waste, individuals can produce nutrient-rich soil for gardening. This decentralized approach reduces reliance on external waste disposal systems and minimizes environmental impact.

This undertaking entails establishing a compost bin or pile in your backyard, making use of kitchen leftovers such as fruit and vegetable peels, coffee grounds, and garden debris. The composting process involves the decomposition of organic matter by microorganisms, producing valuable compost for enriching soil fertility. Additionally, it helps reduce methane emissions from decomposing organic waste in landfills.

In a grid-down scenario, where conventional waste management may be compromised, a Home Composting System becomes even more critical. It offers a sustainable solution to organic waste disposal while empowering individuals to contribute to their own food production. This simple and accessible project aligns with the principles of self-sufficiency and environmental stewardship, making it an essential component of grid survival strategies.

Step 1: Choose a Composting Method

- **Tumbler or Bin:** Decide whether you want to use a compost tumbler or a compost bin. Tumblers are convenient for easy turning, while bins offer simplicity and flexibility.

Step 2: Gather Materials and Tools

Materials:

- **Compost Tumbler or Bin:** Purchase or repurpose a suitable container.
- **Drill with Bits (for bins):** If using a bin, you'll need a drill to create ventilation holes.
- **Brown Material (Dry Leaves, Straw):** Provides carbon and balances the compost.

- **Green Material (Kitchen Scraps, Fresh Yard Waste):** Adds nitrogen to the compost.
- **Garden Soil:** Introduces beneficial microorganisms.
- **Water:** Maintains moisture in the compost.

Tools:

- **Shovel or Pitchfork:** For turning and aerating the compost.
- **Hose or Watering Can:** To include water to the compost.
- **Thermometer (Optional):** Monitors compost temperature.

Step 3: Set Up the Composting Area

- **Choose a Location:** Place your compost tumbler or bin in a well-drained area with good air circulation.
- **Consider Sunlight:** While partial shade is ideal, some sunlight is beneficial for the composting process.

Step 4: Prepare the Compost Bin (for bin users)

- **Drill Ventilation Holes:** If using a bin, drill holes on the sides and bottom for aeration. Space holes evenly to allow air to circulate.

Step 5: Layering Your Compost

- **Base Layer (Brown Material):** Start with a layer of brown material, such as dry leaves or straw, to create a carbon-rich foundation.
- **Second Layer (Green Material):** Include a layer of green material, like kitchen scraps or fresh yard waste, for nitrogen.
- **Third Layer (Garden Soil):** Introduce a layer of garden soil to introduce essential microorganisms.

Step 6: Include Moisture

- **Water Each Layer:** As you include each layer, lightly moisten it with water. The compost needs to have a moisture level similar to that of a squeezed-out sponge.

Step 7: Turn and Mix

- **Turn Regularly:** Turn the compost regularly with a shovel or pitchfork to aerate and speed up the decomposition process.
- **Monitor Moisture:** Ensure the compost remains consistently moist, adjusting with water as needed.

Step 8: Maintain Proper Balance

- **Balancing Brown and Green Material:** Continue adding layers of brown and green material in a balanced ratio. This ensures the right mix of carbon and nitrogen.
- **Avoid Large Chunks:** Chop or shred large materials for faster decomposition.

Step 9: Monitor Compost Temperature (Optional)

- **Use a Thermometer:** If using a compost thermometer, monitor the internal temperature. A well-balanced compost pile heats up as it decomposes.

Step 10: Harvest Your Compost

- **Wait for Maturity:** Compost is ready when it turns dark and has an earthy smell. This process typically takes several weeks to a few months.
- **Sift or Use as Mulch:** Once ready, sift the compost to remove larger particles or use it directly as mulch in your garden.

Step 11: Troubleshooting and Tips

- **Odor Issues:** If your compost smells, it might be too wet or have an imbalance. Include more brown material and turn the compost.
- **Pest Concerns:** Keep meat, dairy, and oily foods out of the compost to avoid attracting pests.
- **Adjusting the Mix:** If the compost is too dry, include water. If it's too wet, include more brown material and turn.

Building a home composting system is a rewarding and sustainable way to manage organic waste while enriching your garden. This guide provides a straightforward process for creating a composting setup that fits your preferences. By following these steps and maintaining a good balance of brown and green materials, you'll be on your way to producing nutrient-rich compost for healthier plants and a greener environment. Happy composting!

Setting Up A Greywater Recycling System: Step by Step Project

A Greywater Recycling System is a no-grid survival project that maximizes water efficiency. It repurposes household wastewater from sinks, showers, and laundry for non-potable uses like irrigation, reducing reliance on fresh water sources. This eco-friendly solution involves diverting greywater through a filtration system, removing impurities, and directing it to the garden or landscape. By recycling water locally, it conserves resources and promotes sustainable living, especially in arid regions where water scarcity is a concern. Implementing a Greywater Recycling System enhances self-sufficiency by decreasing dependency on external water supplies, making it an integral part of off-grid living. Additionally, it aligns with environmental conservation efforts, minimizing the ecological footprint associated with water consumption. As a simple and adaptable off-grid project, it empowers individuals to contribute to water conservation and resilience in the face of unpredictable circumstances.

Step 1: Understand Greywater and Regulations

- **Define Greywater:** Greywater comprises water sourced from bathroom sinks, showers, bathtubs, and washing machines, excluding water from toilets or kitchen sinks.

- **Check Local Regulations:** Before starting, check local regulations and obtain necessary permits. Some areas have specific rules regarding the use of greywater.

Step 2: Assess Your Household Water Usage

- **Identify Greywater Sources:** Determine which fixtures in your home produce greywater and their locations.
- **Estimate Daily Usage:** Calculate the daily amount of greywater generated by these sources to size your recycling system accordingly.

Step 3: Choose a Greywater System Type

- **Diversion System:** Diverts greywater from one source directly to the landscape without storage.
- **Treatment and Storage System:** Filters and stores greywater for later use, allowing for more flexibility in irrigation timing.

Step 4: Gather Materials and Tools

Common Components:

- **Greywater Diverter or Treatment System:** Depending on your chosen system type.
- **Pipe and Fittings:** For transporting greywater.
- **Mulch Basins or Irrigation Lines:** For distributing greywater in the landscape.
- **Filter (if applicable):** Removes debris from greywater.
- **Pump (if applicable):** For pressurized irrigation.

Tools:

- **Shovel and Digging Tools:** For excavation.
- **Pipe Cutter and Wrenches:** For working with plumbing.
- **Tape Measure:** For accurate measurements.
- **Spirit Level:** For ensuring proper slope in pipes.
- **Safety Gear:** Gloves and safety glasses.

Step 5: Design Your Greywater System

- **Map Out Greywater Sources:** Identify where greywater will be collected.
- **Plan Irrigation Zones:** Determine where you'll use the recycled greywater in your landscape.
- **Consider Slope and Gravity:** Design your system to take advantage of gravity flow whenever possible.

Step 6: Install Greywater Diverter or Treatment System

- **Install Diverter:** If using a diversion system, install a greywater diverter at the source (e.g., laundry machine).
- **Connect Treatment System (if applicable):** If using a treatment system, install and connect it according to the manufacturer's guidelines.

Step 7: Lay Out Pipes and Irrigation Lines

- **Connect Pipes:** Use PVC or flexible pipes to transport greywater from the source to the irrigation zones.
- **Install Mulch Basins or Drip Lines:** Place mulch basins or set up drip irrigation lines in the chosen landscape areas.

Step 8: Excavate and Bury Pipes

- **Dig Trenches:** Excavate trenches for burying pipes. Ensure a gentle slope for gravity flow.
- **Lay Pipes:** Place pipes in the trenches, connecting them to the greywater source and irrigation zones.

Step 9: Install Filters and Pumps (if applicable)

- **Include Filters:** Install filters in the greywater line to remove debris. Clean or replace filters regularly.
- **Include Pump (if needed):** If your irrigation zones require pressurized water, install a pump in the system.

Step 10: Test and Adjust the System

- **Run a Test:** Turn on the greywater system and test its functionality. Inspect for leaks and confirm adequate water circulation.

- **Adjust Settings:** Fine-tune settings such as pump pressure and irrigation timing based on system performance.

Step 11: Inform Household Members and Maintain

- **Educate Residents:** Inform household members about the greywater system, including what can and cannot go down drains.
- **Regular Maintenance:** Regularly inspect and maintain the system, cleaning filters and checking for any issues.

Step 12: Monitor Local Regulations and Adapt

- **Stay Informed:** Keep up to date with any changes in local regulations related to greywater use.
- **Adapt as Needed:** If regulations change or you encounter issues, be prepared to adapt your system accordingly.

Setting up a greywater recycling system is a tangible step toward water conservation and sustainable living.

Implementing Organic Waste Digesters: Step by Step Project

Organic Waste Digesters are innovative no-grid survival projects designed to convert organic waste into valuable resources. These digesters utilize microbial activity to break down kitchen scraps, agricultural residues, and other organic materials, producing biogas and nutrient-rich compost. The biogas generated can be used for cooking and heating, providing a sustainable energy source off the grid. Additionally, the resulting compost enhances soil fertility, supporting plant growth for food production. This project promotes self-sufficiency by reducing dependence on traditional energy sources and chemical fertilizers. It is a cost-effective and eco-friendly solution that addresses waste management while contributing to the creation of a closed-loop system, making it an essential component for resilient and sustainable living in off-grid scenarios.

Step 1: Understand Organic Waste Digesters

- **Definition:** Organic waste digesters use microorganisms to break down organic matter into compost.
- **Types:** Choose between aerobic (composting with air) and anaerobic (composting without air) digesters.

Step 2: Gather Materials and Tools

Materials:

- **Container or Bin:** Choose a container suitable for your needs (plastic or metal).
- **Drill with Bits:** For creating ventilation holes (if using aerobic digester).
- **Browns (Dry Leaves, Straw):** Provide carbon for the composting process.
- **Greens (Kitchen Scraps, Green Yard Waste):** Supply nitrogen for the compost.
- **Shovel or Pitchfork:** For turning and aerating the compost.
- **Watering Can or Hose:** To maintain proper moisture levels.
- **Optional: Compost Accelerator or Activator:** Speeds up the composting process.

Tools:

- **Drill with Bits (if using aerobic system):** For creating ventilation holes.
- **Shovel or Pitchfork:** For turning and aerating the compost.

Step 3: Choose a Location for the Digester

- **Select a Shaded Area:** Place the digester in a shaded area to prevent it from drying out too quickly.
- **Consider Accessibility:** Choose a location that is easily accessible for adding materials and turning the compost.

Step 4: Set Up the Container or Bin

- **Drill Ventilation Holes (for Aerobic Digesters):** If using an aerobic system, drill holes in the container to allow air circulation.
- **Elevate the Container (Optional):** Elevate the container slightly to improve drainage.

Step 5: Layer Organic Materials

- **Base Layer (Browns):** Start with a layer of dry leaves or straw as the carbon-rich base.
- **Second Layer (Greens):** Include a layer of kitchen scraps and green yard waste for nitrogen.

Step 6: Include Water and Mix

- **Moisten the Layers:** Water each layer lightly as you include it to the digester. Aim for a damp, sponge-like consistency.
- **Mix the Layers:** Turn the compost with a shovel or pitchfork to mix the materials and enhance aeration.

Step 7: Monitor Moisture and Aeration

- **Check Moisture Levels:** Regularly check the moisture levels in the digester. Include water if it becomes too dry or mix in dry materials if it's too wet.
- **Turn the Compost:** Turn the compost every few days to ensure even decomposition and adequate aeration.

Step 8: Include Organic Waste Regularly

- **Daily Kitchen Scraps:** Dispose of kitchen scraps daily by adding them to the digester.
- **Balance Greens and Browns:** Maintain a balance between green and brown materials to optimize the composting process.

Step 9: Accelerate Composting (Optional)

- **Use Compost Accelerator:** If desired, include a compost accelerator or activator to speed up the decomposition process.

Step 10: Harvest the Compost

- **Wait for Maturity:** Compost is ready when it turns dark, has an earthy smell, and the original materials are no longer recognizable.

- **Sieve or Use as Mulch:** Sieve the compost to remove large particles, or use it directly as mulch in your garden.

Step 11: Troubleshooting and Tips

- **Foul Odor:** If the digester smells bad, it may be too wet or lack aeration. Include more brown materials and turn the compost.
- **Slow Decomposition:** To speed up decomposition, ensure a good balance of greens and browns, and turn the compost regularly.

Step 12: Educate and Share Compost

- **Educate Others:** Share knowledge about organic waste digestion with friends and family.
- **Share Compost:** Share the nutrient-rich compost with neighbors or use it in your garden to promote sustainable practices.

Implementing an organic waste digester is a practical way to manage kitchen scraps and create valuable compost for your garden. This guide provides a simple and effective approach to setting up a digester at home. If you follow these instructions and make composting a regular part of your routine, you will notice that, you contribute to reducing organic waste in landfills and enriching your soil with nutrient-rich compost. Happy composting!

Chapter 6:

Sustainable Food Gardens

Introduction: Getting Started with Permaculture, Key Concepts

Permaculture, a condensed term for permanent agriculture or permanent culture, entails a comprehensive methodology for crafting systems that are both sustainable and regenerative, in alignment with the principles of nature. Developed by Bill Mollison and David Holmgren in the 1970s, permaculture integrates ecological principles, traditional wisdom, and innovative thinking to create resilient and productive ecosystems.

Understanding Permaculture

At its core, permaculture is about creating harmonious and enduring systems that mimic the diversity, stability, and resilience of natural ecosystems. It goes beyond gardening and agriculture, encompassing all aspects of human life, from energy and water systems to community dynamics and economic structures. Permaculture encourages a shift from a linear, resource-depleting mindset to one that embraces circular, sustainable practices.

Key Principles of Permaculture

1. **Observation and Interaction:** Permaculture starts with keen observation of natural patterns and interactions. By understanding the land, climate, and ecosystem dynamics, practitioners can design systems that work with, not against, the forces at play.

2. **Catch and Store Energy:** Permaculture harnesses renewable energy sources, both natural and human-made, to meet needs sustainably. This includes strategies like capturing rainwater, utilizing solar energy, and storing excess energy for future use.

3. **Obtain a Yield:** A fundamental principle is ensuring that systems produce yields of value. This may include food crops, building materials, or even social benefits. By obtaining a yield, the system becomes more self-sustaining and rewarding.

4. **Apply Self-Regulation and Accept Feedback:** Permaculture systems are designed to self-regulate and adapt. Learning from feedback, whether from the environment or community, is crucial for making informed adjustments and fostering resilience.

5. **Use and Value Renewable Resources and Services:** Permaculture prioritizes the use of renewable resources over non-renewable ones. This includes maximizing the use of sunlight, wind, and natural cycles while minimizing reliance on finite resources.

6. **Produce No Waste:** Waste is seen as a resource out of place. Permaculture aims to create closed-loop systems where outputs from one element become inputs for another, minimizing waste and promoting efficiency.

7. **Design from Patterns to Details:** Permaculture design starts with understanding broad patterns and functions before delving into specifics. This approach ensures that the design is coherent, integrated, and aligns with the natural order.

8. **Integrate Rather Than Segregate:** By integrating diverse elements, permaculture systems enhance the overall synergy. Polycultures, mixed plantings, and diverse habitats create resilient ecosystems where each element serves multiple functions.

9. **Use Small and Slow Solutions:** Favoring small-scale, gradual changes over large, abrupt ones is a permaculture strategy. Small interventions are easier to manage, observe, and adjust, leading to more sustainable and lasting results.

10. **Use and Value Diversity:** Diversity is a strength in permaculture. Diverse plant and animal species contribute to ecosystem stability, resilience, and increased productivity. This principle extends to cultural and social diversity as well.

11. **Use Edges and Value the Marginal:** The edges of systems often exhibit increased diversity and productivity. Permaculture design maximizes the potential of these zones, recognizing that innovation and abundance often occur at the margins.

12. **Creatively Use and Respond to Change:** Change is inevitable, and permaculture embraces it. By creatively responding to changes in the environment or society, permaculturists can adapt and thrive in dynamic conditions.

Designing with Zones and Sectors

Permaculture design is organized using zones and sectors. Zones represent areas of activity, with those requiring frequent attention (like a kitchen garden) placed close to the home, while less intensively managed zones extend outward. Sectors consider external influences, such as sunlight, wind, and water flow, guiding the placement of elements within the design.

Permaculture Ethics

Permaculture is guided by three core ethics:

- **Earth Care:** Respect and care for the Earth and its ecosystems.
- **People Care:** Promote the well-being of individuals, communities, and future generations.
- **Fair Share (or Return of Surplus):** Share resources and ensure that surplus benefits others and the Earth.

Permaculture is more than a set of gardening techniques; it's a philosophy and a way of life. By understanding and applying its key concepts, individuals can create sustainable, resilient, and regenerative systems that contribute to the well-being of the planet and its inhabitants. Whether you're a gardener, farmer, or urban dweller, embracing permaculture principles offers a path to living in harmony with nature and fostering a more sustainable and regenerative future.

Designing and Implementing A Permaculture Garden: Step by Step Project

A permaculture garden is a sustainable and resilient no-grid survival project that focuses on designing ecosystems inspired by natural patterns. By integrating diverse plants and utilizing companion planting, permaculture gardens maximize yield while minimizing inputs. Emphasizing organic practices and water conservation, these gardens foster self-sufficiency. Techniques like mulching and composting enhance soil fertility, reducing dependence on external resources. Permaculture principles guide the layout, promoting harmony between elements. This low-maintenance approach ensures long-term productivity, making it an ideal no-grid survival project. It fosters biodiversity, attracting beneficial insects and wildlife, contributing to a balanced ecosystem. With an emphasis on perennial crops, permaculture gardens provide a continuous yield, enhancing their resilience to external disruptions. By mimicking nature's wisdom, permaculture gardens exemplify a holistic and regenerative approach to sustainable living, making them an excellent choice for those seeking self-reliance without relying on conventional grids.

Step 1: Site Analysis and Observation

- **Understand Sun and Wind Patterns:** Observe sunlight and wind patterns to identify microclimates and plan accordingly.
- **Map Water Flow:** Determine how water flows across the site during rainfall and consider designing swales or rain gardens.
- **Soil Assessment:** Analyze soil composition, texture, and fertility. This helps in choosing suitable plants and designing soil-enhancing strategies.
- **Identify Existing Plants and Features:** Note existing plants, trees, and landscape features. Consider how they can be integrated into the permaculture design.

Step 2: Set Design Goals and Zones

- **Define Your Goals:** Determine your garden's primary purpose, whether it's food production, habitat creation, or aesthetic beauty.

- **Establish Zones:** Divide the garden into zones based on frequency of use and management. Place high-maintenance elements closer to your home.

Step 3: Choose Suitable Plants

- **Select Perennial Plants:** Prioritize perennial plants that offer long-term benefits and require less maintenance.
- **Consider Guild Planting:** Design plant guilds where companion plants support each other. For example, nitrogen-fixing plants near nutrient-demanding crops.

Step 4: Design Pathways and Access Points

- **Create Access Paths:** Plan pathways to provide easy access while ensuring efficient use of space.
- **Incorporate Gathering Spaces:** Designate spaces for gathering, seating, or outdoor activities within the garden.

Step 5: Implement Water Harvesting Techniques

- **Install Rain Barrels:** Set up rain barrels to collect and store rainwater for irrigation.
- **Design Swales or Contour Planting:** Utilize swales or contour planting to slow water runoff and enhance water absorption.

Step 6: Use Vertical Gardening Strategies

- **Install Trellises and Arbors:** Create vertical growing spaces for climbing plants and vines.
- **Consider Vertical Planting Systems:** Use vertical gardening solutions like living walls or vertical planters.

Step 7: Integrate Composting and Mulching Systems

- **Create Compost Bins or Piles:** Designate an area for composting kitchen waste and garden debris.
- **Mulch Garden Beds:** Apply mulch to retain moisture, suppress weeds, and improve soil fertility.

Step 8: Implement Companion Planting

- **Choose Companion Plants:** Select plants that mutually benefit each other, such as repelling pests or enhancing soil fertility.
- **Diversify Plant Species:** Promote biodiversity by planting a variety of species to create a resilient ecosystem.

Step 9: Install Permaculture Elements

- **Incorporate Permaculture Features:** Integrate elements like herb spirals, keyhole beds, or hügelkultur mounds for added diversity and function.
- **Build a Wildlife Habitat:** Design spaces to attract beneficial wildlife, such as pollinators and pest predators.

Step 10: Create a Maintenance Plan

- **Establish a Routine:** Develop a maintenance routine for tasks like pruning, harvesting, and pest control.
- **Monitor Soil Health:** Regularly assess soil health and make adjustments as needed, such as adding compost or adjusting pH.

Step 11: Educate and Share Knowledge

- **Educate Others:** Share permaculture knowledge with neighbors, friends, and community members.
- **Promote Sustainable Practices:** Encourage sustainable gardening practices within your community.

Designing and implementing a permaculture garden is a fulfilling journey toward sustainable living. By incorporating these steps and principles, you create a resilient and productive space that harmonizes with nature. A permaculture garden not only provides fresh produce but also contributes to biodiversity, soil health, and a more sustainable way of living. Enjoy the abundance and connection with the natural world that your permaculture garden brings.

Creating High-Yield Raised Bed Gardens: Step by Step Project

High-Yield Raised Bed Gardens are no-grid survival projects that maximize limited space for efficient food production. These raised beds, elevated above ground, enhance soil drainage and warmth, extending the growing season. Using simple materials like wood or concrete blocks, they are cost-effective and customizable to fit various locations. Incorporating companion planting techniques further boosts yields, as certain plants naturally complement each other, deterring pests and enhancing nutrient uptake. With minimal water and fertilizer requirements, these gardens are sustainable and low-maintenance. Additionally, raised beds provide better control over soil quality, reducing the need for external amendments. Ideal for urban or small-scale environments, these gardens empower individuals to cultivate their own fresh produce, promoting self-sufficiency and resilience in times of crisis.

Step 1: Planning and Design

- **Determine Bed Dimensions:** Determine the dimensions of your raised beds by considering the available space and the convenience of maintenance.
- **Choose a Suitable Location:** Select a sunny location with good drainage. Consider proximity to water sources for irrigation.
- **Sketch the Layout:** Create a rough sketch or plan of your garden layout, indicating the placement and dimensions of each raised bed.

Step 2: Gather Materials and Tools

Materials:

- **Lumber or Timber:** Choose rot-resistant wood like cedar or redwood. Example: 2x6 or 2x8 boards.
- **Wood Screws or Nails:** For assembling the raised bed frames.
- **Garden Soil:** A high-quality mix of topsoil, compost, and organic matter.
- **Cardboard or Newspaper:** For weed suppression under the raised beds.
- **Hardware Cloth (Optional):** To deter burrowing pests.
- **Landscaping Fabric (Optional):** To prevent weed growth.
- **Mulch:** For pathways between beds.

Tools:

- **Power Drill or Screwdriver:** For assembling the raised bed frames.
- **Saw:** To cut the lumber to the desired lengths.
- **Level:** To ensure the beds are even.
- **Shovel:** For preparing the site and filling the beds.
- **Tape Measure:** For accurate measurements.
- **Staple Gun (Optional):** For securing landscaping fabric.

Step 3: Site Preparation

- **Clear the Area:** Remove grass, weeds, or debris from the designated area.
- **Level the Ground:** Ensure the ground is level by removing high spots and filling in low spots.
- **Lay Cardboard or Newspaper:** Place cardboard or several layers of newspaper over the cleared area to suppress weeds.

Step 4: Building the Raised Bed Frames

- **Cut Lumber to Size:** Employ a saw to trim the lumber to the preferred dimensions for the sides of the raised bed.
- **Assemble Frames:** Attach the cut lumber to form rectangular frames. Use screws or nails to secure the corners.
- **Optional: Include Hardware Cloth:** Attach hardware cloth to the bottom of the frame to deter burrowing pests.

Step 5: Install Raised Beds

- **Place Frames on Prepared Site:** Set the assembled frames on top of the cardboard or newspaper.
- **Level the Beds:** Use a level to ensure the beds are even.
- **Optional: Install Landscaping Fabric:** If using landscaping fabric, lay it on the bottom of the frame to further suppress weeds.

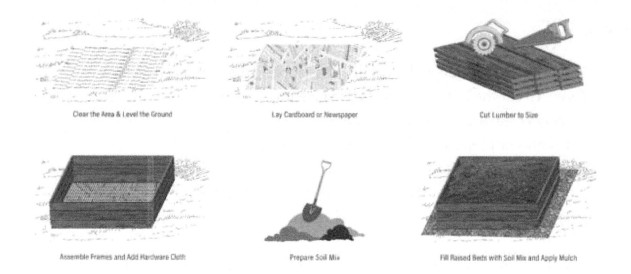

Clear the Area & Level the Ground

Lay Cardboard or Newspaper

Cut Lumber to Size

Assemble Frames and Add Hardware Cloth

Prepare Soil Mix

Fill Raised Beds with Soil Mix and Apply Mulch

Step 6: Fill Raised Beds with Soil Mix

- **Prepare Soil Mix:** Mix garden soil, compost, and organic matter in a ratio suitable for your plants.
- **Fill the Beds:** Fill the raised beds with the prepared soil mix, ensuring it is evenly distributed.
- **Shape the Soil:** Shape the soil surface within the bed to create planting mounds or rows.

Step 7: Mulch Pathways Between Beds

- **Apply Mulch:** Spread mulch along the pathways between the raised beds. This helps with weed control and moisture retention.
- **Create Clear Pathways:** Ensure clear and defined pathways for easy access and maintenance.

Step 8: Planting in the Raised Beds

- **Plan Your Planting Layout:** Arrange plants within each raised bed based on their spacing and sunlight requirements.
- **Plant Seedlings or Seeds:** Plant your chosen crops in the prepared soil, following recommended planting depths and spacing.
- **Water Thoroughly:** Ensure that the recently planted seeds or seedlings receive a generous watering.

Step 9: Implementing Irrigation Systems (Optional)

- **Drip Irrigation:** Contemplate the installation of a drip irrigation system to enhance water efficiency and precision in watering.
- **Soaker Hoses:** Alternatively, use soaker hoses to ensure even moisture distribution.

Step 10: Implementing Support Structures (Optional)

- **Install Trellises or Supports:** For vertical gardening, install trellises or supports for climbing plants like tomatoes or beans.
- **Include Plant Markers:** Label plants using markers or signs for easy identification.

Step 11: Regular Maintenance and Care

- **Weeding:** Keep an eye on weeds and remove them regularly.
- **Mulching:** Replenish mulch as needed to maintain weed suppression and moisture retention.
- **Fertilizing:** Follow a fertilization schedule based on the needs of your plants.

By following these steps, you've created a high-yield raised bed garden that optimizes space, enhances soil quality, and simplifies gardening tasks. The raised beds provide an organized and accessible growing environment, promoting successful cultivation and bountiful harvests. Enjoy the fruits of your labor and the benefits of a well-designed and productive garden.

Developing an Efficient Drip Irrigation System: Step by Step Project

A Drip Irrigation System is a crucial component of off-grid survival, ensuring efficient water usage in agriculture. This endeavor entails establishing a system of tubes and emitters designed to efficiently deliver water directly to the roots of plants, thereby reducing unnecessary water wastage. The system operates on low pressure, making it suitable for areas with limited water resources. It conserves water, reduces labor, and enhances crop yield, making it ideal for self-sustenance. Components include pipes, drip tape, and emitters, which can be easily assembled. Solar-powered pumps or gravity feed systems can be integrated, eliminating the need for a consistent power supply. Drip irrigation accommodates various crop types and soil conditions, adapting to off-grid environments. Its simplicity, affordability, and water-saving features make it an indispensable project for resilient, sustainable agriculture in remote locations.

Step 1: Planning and Design

- **Assess Your Garden Layout:** Assess the dimensions, configuration, and arrangement of your garden to decide where to position drip lines and emitters.
- **Identify Water Source:** Locate a reliable water source, such as a faucet or hose connection, for your drip irrigation system.
- **Sketch Your Garden Plan:** Sketch a preliminary design for your garden, indicating the placement of plants, pathways, and the location of the water source.

Step 2: Gather Materials and Tools

Materials:

- **Drip Tubing:** Main tubing that carries water to various parts of the garden.
- **Drip Emitters:** Devices that release water directly to plants.
- **Drip Connectors and Fittings:** For connecting tubing and emitters.
- **Stakes or Hold-Downs:** Secures tubing and prevents movement.
- **Filter:** Prevents clogging of emitters.
- **Pressure Regulator:** Maintains consistent water pressure.
- **Backflow Preventer:** Stops water from flowing back into the main water supply.
- **Timer:** Automates watering schedules.

Tools:

- **Scissors or Tubing Cutter:** For cutting drip tubing.
- **Punch Tool:** Creates holes for emitters and connectors.
- **Adjustable Wrench:** Tightens fittings securely.
- **Tape Measure:** For accurate measurements.

Step 3: Measure and Cut Drip Tubing

- **Measure Garden Paths:** Measure the distances between plants and along garden pathways to determine the length of drip tubing needed.
- **Cut Tubing:** Use scissors or a tubing cutter to cut the drip tubing to the required lengths.

Step 4: Lay Out Drip Tubing

- **Start at the Water Source:** Begin laying out the drip tubing from the water source, ensuring it reaches all parts of the garden.
- **Secure Tubing with Stakes:** Use stakes or hold-downs to secure the tubing in place along pathways and around plants.

Step 5: Install Emitters and Connectors

- **Use Punch Tool:** Utilize a punch tool to establish openings in the drip tubing at the locations of the plants.
- **Insert Connectors:** Insert connectors into the holes to attach drip emitters or additional tubing.
- **Connect Emitters:** Attach drip emitters to the connectors, ensuring a secure fit.

Step 6: Install Filters, Pressure Regulator, and Backflow Preventer

- **Connect Filter:** Install a filter at the beginning of the drip system to prevent clogging. Connect it to the water source.
- **Attach Pressure Regulator:** Connect a pressure regulator to maintain consistent water pressure, improving the efficiency of the system.
- **Install Backflow Preventer:** Install a backflow preventer to stop water from flowing back into the main water supply.

Step 7: Connect Tubing to Water Source

- **Attach Tubing to Faucet or Hose Bib:** Connect the main drip tubing to the water source, securing it tightly with a wrench.
- **Use Timer for Automation:** If desired, install a timer between the faucet and drip system for automated watering schedules.

Step 8: Test and Adjust the System

- **Turn on Water Source:** Turn on the water source and observe the system for leaks, ensuring water flows to all emitters.
- **Adjust Emitters and Flow Rates:** Adjust the position of emitters and their flow rates to meet the watering needs of different plants.

- **Check Timer Settings:** If using a timer, verify and adjust the settings for watering frequency and duration.

Step 9: Mulch and Conceal Tubing (Optional)

- **Apply Mulch:** Cover the drip tubing with mulch to protect it from sunlight and promote water retention.
- **Conceal Tubing:** Bury tubing under a thin layer of soil or decorative materials for a more aesthetic appearance.

Step 10: Regular Maintenance

- **Inspect System Periodically:** Check the system regularly for clogs, leaks, or damaged components.
- **Clean Filters:** Clean filters as needed to maintain efficient water flow.
- **Adjust for Seasonal Changes:** Adjust watering schedules and emitters based on seasonal changes in plant water requirements.

By following these steps, you've successfully developed an efficient drip irrigation system for your garden. This system minimizes water wastage, ensures targeted watering, and promotes healthy plant growth.

Chapter 7:

Preserving and Storing Food

Introduction: The Essentials of Food Preservation Methods

In a world where access to fresh produce may be limited by season or circumstances, the art and science of food preservation play an important role in ensuring a consistent food supply. Food preservation involves various techniques that extend the shelf life of perishable foods, maintaining their nutritional value and taste. This introduction explores the essentials of food preservation methods, from ancient practices to modern innovations, providing a comprehensive overview of the techniques that have sustained communities throughout history.

Understanding the Need for Food Preservation

Throughout human history, communities faced the challenge of securing a stable food supply, especially during periods of scarcity or in regions with distinct seasons. The need to preserve food arose from the desire to store surplus harvests for times when fresh produce was not readily available. This led to the development of various preservation methods that have evolved and diversified over time.

Ancient Preservation Methods

- **Drying:** Drying, one of the ancient techniques, entails eliminating moisture from food to hinder the proliferation of microorganisms. Ancient civilizations used sunlight, air, or smoke to dry fruits, vegetables, and meats.
- **Fermentation:** Utilizing the inherent capabilities of bacteria and yeast, fermentation transforms sugars and starches present in food into acids or alcohol. This process not only preserves food but also imparts unique flavors. Examples include sauerkraut, kimchi, and pickles.

- **Curing and Smoking:** Curing involves treating food with salt, sugar, or nitrates to draw out moisture and inhibit bacterial growth. Smoking, often combined with curing, adds flavor and further extends the shelf life of meats and fish.
- **Root Cellaring:** In regions with cold climates, people traditionally stored root vegetables like potatoes, carrots, and turnips in cool, underground root cellars to prevent spoilage.

Introduction of Modern Preservation Techniques

- **Canning:** Developed in the 19th century, canning involves sealing food in airtight containers and heat-processing them to destroy microorganisms. This technique safeguards an extensive array of food items, encompassing fruits, vegetables, and meats.
- **Refrigeration:** The advent of refrigeration revolutionized food preservation by slowing down the growth of spoilage-causing bacteria. Refrigerators and freezers allow for the safe storage of perishable items for extended periods.
- **Freezing:** Preserving food at low temperatures hinders the development of microorganisms and enzymatic reactions responsible for causing spoilage. It is a widely used method for preserving fruits, vegetables, meats, and prepared meals.
- **Vacuum Packing:** Vacuum packing removes air from the packaging, inhibiting the growth of aerobic bacteria and preventing oxidation. This method is commonly used for preserving a variety of foods, including deli meats and cheese.

Innovations in Food Preservation

- **High-Pressure Processing (HPP):** HPP uses high-pressure water to inactivate bacteria, yeasts, molds, and enzymes without the need for high temperatures. It maintains the freshness and nutritional excellence of items such as juices, deli meats, and guacamole.
- **Modified Atmosphere Packaging (MAP):** MAP alters the composition of the air surrounding food products to slow down deterioration. It is frequently employed to package fresh fruits, vegetables, meat, and seafood.

- **Dehydration Technologies:** Advanced dehydration methods, such as freeze-drying and spray-drying, preserve food by removing moisture without compromising texture or nutritional value. These techniques are employed for producing instant coffee, powdered fruits, and astronaut food.
- **Electroporation:** Electroporation involves applying electrical pulses to food, creating temporary pores in cell membranes. This method increases the penetration of preservatives and extends the shelf life of certain products.

Considerations for Choosing Preservation Methods

- **Nature of the Food:** Different foods respond better to specific preservation methods. For example, fruits may be well-suited for canning, while herbs might benefit from drying.
- **Nutritional Content:** Some preservation methods better retain the nutritional value of foods than others. For instance, freezing is known for preserving vitamins in fruits and vegetables.
- **Flavor and Texture:** Preservation methods can impact the flavor and texture of foods. Fermented foods, for example, often acquire unique and desirable tastes during the preservation process.
- **Cost and Accessibility:** The cost of equipment and the availability of resources, such as refrigeration or canning supplies, can influence the choice of preservation methods for individuals or communities.

In the pursuit of securing a consistent and dependable food source, the various techniques of preserving food have evolved into essential tools for individuals, communities, and industries alike. From time-honored practices rooted in tradition to cutting-edge technologies that push the boundaries of what is possible, the world of food preservation continues to evolve. This introduction aims to provide a broad understanding of the essentials, enabling individuals to navigate the choices available and make informed decisions about how best to preserve and enjoy the bounty of the harvest, year-round.

Constructing A Root Cellar for Food Storage: Step by Step Project

A root cellar is a fundamental component of a no-grid survival project, providing essential food storage without reliance on external power sources. This underground storage facility maintains a cool, consistent temperature, prolonging the freshness of fruits, vegetables, and preserves. Its construction involves digging a hole, reinforcing walls, and implementing proper ventilation to prevent spoilage. This self-sustaining solution ensures a year-round food supply, reducing dependence on refrigeration or electricity. In times of crisis, a well-designed root cellar becomes a strategic asset, allowing families to stockpile food and minimize waste. The simplicity of this project, rooted in traditional wisdom, empowers individuals to take control of their sustenance, fostering resilience and self-sufficiency in challenging situations.

Step 1: Planning and Site Selection

- **Choose an Appropriate Location:** Select a site for your root cellar that is away from direct sunlight, well-drained, and has good ventilation.
- **Evaluate Soil Conditions:** Assess the soil conditions to ensure proper drainage and consider the water table level.
- **Determine the Size:** Decide on the size of your root cellar based on the amount of produce you plan to store and available space.

Step 2: Excavation and Foundation

- **Excavate the Site:** Dig a hole in the chosen location, considering the depth needed for your cellar. The typical depth ranges from 4 to 8 feet.
- **Level the Floor:** Level the floor of the excavation site to ensure a flat foundation.
- **Construct a Foundation:** Build a sturdy foundation using concrete blocks or poured concrete to support the structure.

Step 3: Constructing Walls and Ceiling

- **Frame the Walls:** Frame the walls of your root cellar using pressure-treated lumber. Ensure proper bracing for stability.

- **Install Insulation:** Attach insulation material to the interior walls to regulate temperature and humidity. Common choices include foam board insulation.
- **Construct a Ventilation System:** Incorporate a ventilation system, such as PVC pipes or vents, to let for fresh air circulation.
- **Build the Ceiling:** Construct a ceiling using lumber and insulation. Ensure it is well-insulated to maintain a consistent temperature.

Step 4: Installing a Door and Entrance

- **Install a Sturdy Door:** Choose a well-insulated and weather-sealed door. Install it securely to maintain the cellar's temperature and humidity levels.
- **Create an Entrance Ramp:** Build a ramp leading into the root cellar, making it easy to transport produce in and out.

Step 5: Adding Shelves and Storage Bins

- **Install Shelves:** Build shelves along the walls to maximize storage space. Use materials that can withstand cool and humid conditions.
- **Consider Sliding Storage Bins:** For root vegetables like potatoes and carrots, incorporate sliding storage bins to optimize space and ease access.

Step 6: Ventilation and Air Circulation

- **Install Ventilation Tubes:** Place ventilation tubes or pipes that extend from the outside into the cellar to ensure a continuous flow of fresh air.
- **Include Adjustable Vents:** Install adjustable vents to control airflow and regulate humidity levels within the root cellar.

Step 7: Lighting and Electrical Considerations

- **Provide Adequate Lighting:** Install LED lighting to ensure visibility inside the cellar. Avoid using incandescent bulbs that generate heat.
- **Consider Electrical Outlets:** Include electrical outlets if you plan to use the space for additional purposes like storing canned goods or tools.

Step 8: Insulating the Roof and Walls

- **Insulate the Roof:** Include insulation material to the roof structure to prevent temperature fluctuations and maintain a cool environment.
- **Insulate Exterior Walls:** Apply insulation material to the exterior walls to create a barrier between the cellar's interior and the external environment.

Step 9: Sealing Gaps and Cracks

- **Seal Gaps and Cracks:** Ensure airtight conditions by sealing any gaps or cracks in the walls, ceiling, and around the door.
- **Apply Weather Stripping:** Use weather stripping around the door to prevent the entry of outside air.

Step 10: Final Inspection and Testing

- **Check for Proper Ventilation:** Confirm that the ventilation system is functioning correctly by testing the airflow and adjusting vents as needed.
- **Monitor Temperature and Humidity:** Utilize a thermometer and hygrometer for tracking and fine-tuning the temperature and humidity levels within the root cellar.
- **Test the Door Seal:** Ensure the door seals tightly when closed, preventing the escape of cool air.

Step 11: Landscaping and Concealment (Optional)

- **Include Landscaping Around the Entrance:** Landscape the area around the entrance to improve aesthetics and provide natural camouflage.
- **Consider Concealing the Entrance:** If desired, create a structure or use natural elements to conceal the entrance, adding an additional layer of security.

By following these steps, you've successfully constructed a root cellar, a time-honored method for preserving fruits, vegetables, and other perishables. This underground storage space provides an ideal environment for extending the shelf life of your harvest, reducing food waste, and ensuring a bountiful supply of fresh produce throughout the seasons. Enjoy the fruits of your preservation efforts and the satisfaction of creating a sustainable and efficient storage solution.

Building A Solar Dehydrator for Food Preservation: Step by Step Project

The Solar Dehydrator for Food Preservation is a practical, off-grid survival project that harnesses the power of the sun to preserve food. This simple yet effective device uses solar energy to remove moisture from fruits, vegetables, and herbs, extending their shelf life without the need for electricity. By constructing a wooden or metal frame and covering it with a transparent material, such as plastic or glass, the dehydrator creates a greenhouse effect. Inside, trays hold sliced produce, allowing the sun's heat to circulate and gradually dehydrate the food. This low-cost solution ensures a sustainable and energy-efficient method for preserving surplus harvests, reducing dependence on electricity and conventional food preservation methods. Ideal for remote or off-grid locations, the Solar Dehydrator promotes self-sufficiency, enabling individuals or communities to store and enjoy homegrown produce year-round.

Step 1: Planning and Design

- **Determine Size and Capacity:** Decide on the size of your solar dehydrator based on the quantity of food you plan to preserve.
- **Sketch the Design:** Create a detailed sketch of your solar dehydrator, including dimensions and placement of key components.
- **Select Suitable Materials:** Choose weather-resistant and durable materials for the frame, trays, and cover. Common choices include wood, aluminum, and clear plastic.

Step 2: Materials and Tools

Materials:

- **Wooden Frame or Plywood Sheets:** For constructing the frame.
- **Aluminum or Steel Mesh Sheets:** To create drying trays.
- **Clear Plastic Sheets or Plexiglas:** For the cover.
- **Hinges and Latches:** To attach the cover securely.
- **Weather-resistant Screws and Nails:** For assembling the frame and trays.
- **Black Paint or Heat-Absorbing Material:** To enhance heat absorption.

- **Thermometer and Hygrometer:** For monitoring temperature and humidity.
- **Weather-Resistant Sealant or Caulk:** To seal gaps and joints.

Tools:

- **Circular Saw or Handsaw:** For cutting wood and other materials.
- **Screwdriver and/or Drill:** For assembling the frame and attaching components.
- **Measuring Tape and Square:** For accurate measurements and alignment.
- **Paintbrush:** For applying black paint or heat-absorbing material.
- **Work Gloves and Safety Glasses:** For safety during construction.

Step 3: Building the Frame

- **Cut Frame Components:** Cut the wooden frame components according to your design using a circular saw or handsaw.
- **Assemble the Frame:** Construct the frame by connecting the cut pieces with screws, ensuring it is both robust and adequately supported.
- **Include Support Legs:** If necessary, attach support legs to elevate the dehydrator for better exposure to sunlight.

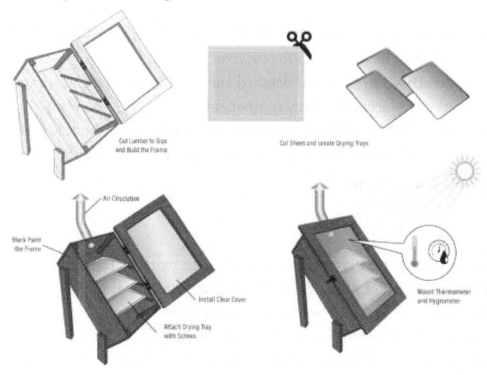

Step 4: Creating Drying Trays

- **Cut Mesh Sheets:** Cut aluminum or steel mesh sheets to fit the dimensions of the frame, creating multiple drying trays.
- **Secure Mesh to Frames:** Attach the mesh sheets to the frames using screws, ensuring they are firmly secured.
- **Allow for Air Circulation:** Ensure there is sufficient space between the mesh and the frame for air circulation around the food.

Step 5: Painting for Heat Absorption

- **Apply Black Paint or Material:** Paint the interior surfaces of the frame with black paint or apply a heat-absorbing material. This enhances the absorption of solar heat.
- **Allow to Dry:** Let the paint or material dry completely before moving on to the next steps.

Step 6: Installing Clear Cover

- **Cut Clear Plastic Sheets:** Cut clear plastic sheets or Plexiglas to the dimensions of the frame, creating a cover.
- **Attach Hinges:** Attach hinges to one side of the frame and the corresponding edge of the cover to create a hinged opening.
- **Install Latches:** Install latches on the opposite side to secure the cover in place during operation.

Step 7: Mounting Thermometer and Hygrometer

- **Position Instruments:** Place a thermometer and hygrometer inside the dehydrator to monitor temperature and humidity levels.
- **Secure Instruments:** Secure the instruments in a location where they are easily visible and accessible.

Step 8: Sealing Gaps and Joints

- **Apply Sealant or Caulk:** Seal any gaps or joints in the frame, cover, and trays using weather-resistant sealant or caulk.

- **Ensure Airtight Seal:** Create an airtight seal to prevent heat loss and maintain optimal drying conditions.

Step 9: Testing and Adjusting

- **Place in Sunlight:** Position the solar dehydrator in direct sunlight, preferably facing south for maximum exposure.
- **Monitor Temperature:** Monitor the temperature inside the dehydrator and adjust the angle of the cover to regulate heat.
- **Adjust Ventilation:** Fine-tune ventilation by partially opening or closing the cover to maintain ideal humidity levels.

Step 10: Using Your Solar Dehydrator

- **Load Drying Trays:** Arrange fruits, vegetables, or herbs on the drying trays, ensuring proper spacing for air circulation.
- **Close Cover Securely:** Close the cover securely and latch it in place during the drying process.
- **Monitor and Rotate:** Regularly check the progress of drying, rotate trays if needed, and adjust the cover for optimal drying conditions.

Congratulations! You've successfully built a solar dehydrator, harnessing the power of the sun to preserve your harvest efficiently and sustainably. This DIY project not only allows you to enjoy the benefits of solar food drying but also contributes to reducing energy consumption. Embrace the art of solar-powered food preservation and savor the flavors of your home-dried fruits, vegetables, and herbs throughout the seasons.

Methods for Fermenting and Pickling at Home

Fermenting and pickling are age-old techniques that have been used for centuries to preserve and enhance the flavors of various foods. These methods not only extend the shelf life of fresh produce but also introduce unique and tangy tastes to culinary creations.

Understanding Fermentation

Fermentation is a natural and transformative process where microorganisms, such as bacteria and yeast, break down sugars and starches in food into alcohol or acids. This not only acts as a preservation method but also enhances the nutritional content and flavor of the food. Here are popular methods for fermenting at home:

1. *Vegetable Fermentation*

Ingredients:

- Vegetables (cabbage, cucumbers, carrots, etc.)
- Salt (non-iodized)
- Spices and herbs (optional)

Steps:

1. **Prepare Vegetables:** Clean and chop vegetables into desired sizes.

2. **Create Brine:** Dissolve salt in water to create a brine solution.

3. **Pack in Jars:** Place vegetables in clean, sterilized jars and cover with the brine.

4. **Weight Down Vegetables:** Use a weight or cabbage leaf to keep vegetables submerged.

5. **Fermentation Period:** Let jars undergo fermentation at room temperature for a duration ranging from a few days to several weeks, depending on the desired degree of fermentation.

6. **Taste and Store:** Taste the fermented vegetables and, once satisfied, store them in the refrigerator or a cool cellar.

2. *Kombucha Fermentation*

Ingredients:

- Black or green tea
- Sugar
- SCOBY (Symbiotic Culture of Bacteria and Yeast)
- Starter tea (from a previous batch)

Steps:

1. **Brew Tea:** Steep tea leaves in hot water and dissolve sugar to create a sweet tea mixture.

2. **Cool and Include SCOBY:** Allow the tea to cool, then include the SCOBY and starter tea.

3. **Fermentation Period:** Cover with a cloth and let it ferment for 7-30 days.

4. **Strain and Bottle:** Strain out the SCOBY and bottle the kombucha.

5. **Secondary Fermentation (Optional):** Include fruits or flavors and let it ferment for an additional period.

6. **Carbonation:** Seal bottles for a few more days to develop natural carbonation.

7. **Refrigerate:** Once satisfied with the taste, refrigerate to slow down fermentation.

Understanding Pickling

Pickling involves preserving food by immersing it in a solution of vinegar, salt, and spices. This process imparts a distinctive tangy flavor to the food and extends its shelf life. Here are methods for pickling at home:

1. Quick Pickling

Ingredients:

- Vegetables (cucumbers, onions, radishes, etc.)
- Vinegar (white or apple cider)
- Water
- Salt
- Sugar
- Spices and herbs

Steps:

1. **Prepare Vegetables:** Clean and slice vegetables thinly.

2. **Create Pickling Liquid:** Blend vinegar, water, salt, sugar, and desired spices in a saucepan.

3. **Boil Pickling Liquid:** Bring the mixture to a boil and simmer until sugar and salt dissolve.

4. **Pack Jars:** Place vegetables in sterilized jars and pour the hot liquid over them.

5. **Cool and Refrigerate:** Allow the jars to cool, then refrigerate for a few hours before consuming.

6. **Quick Enjoyment:** Quick pickles are ready to eat within a day but can be stored for up to a few weeks.

2. Traditional Pickling

Ingredients:

- Vegetables (cucumbers, beets, carrots, etc.)
- Vinegar (white or apple cider)
- Water
- Salt
- Sugar
- Pickling spices (mustard seeds, coriander, dill, etc.)

Steps:

1. **Prepare Vegetables:** Clean and cut vegetables into desired shapes.

2. **Create Brine:** Blend vinegar, water, salt, sugar, and pickling spices in a saucepan to create a brine solution.

3. **Boil Brine:** Bring the brine to a boil, ensuring sugar and salt are dissolved.

4. **Pack Jars:** Place vegetables in sterilized jars and pour the hot brine over them.

5. **Seal Jars:** Seal the jars with lids and bands.

6. **Cool and Store:** Let the jars cool down to room temperature before placing them in a cool, dark location for storage.

7. **Wait for Flavor Development:** Traditional pickles may take several weeks to develop their full flavor.

Tips for Success in Fermenting and Pickling

1. **Use Fresh and Quality Produce:** Start with fresh and high-quality vegetables, fruits, or tea leaves for better results.

2. **Sterilize Equipment:** Ensure all jars, lids, and utensils are thoroughly cleaned and sterilized to prevent contamination.

3. **Experiment with Flavors:** Explore different spices, herbs, and additional flavorings to create unique and personalized ferments and pickles.

4. **Monitor Temperature:** Maintain an appropriate temperature for fermentation, usually around 70°F (21°C).

5. **Be Patient:** Fermentation and pickling take time. Allow the process to unfold naturally for the best results.

6. **Adjust Salt and Sugar Levels:** Adjust the levels of salt and sugar according to your personal taste preferences.

Embarking on the journey of fermenting and pickling at home opens up a world of culinary creativity and preservation. These methods not only include depth and character to your meals but also provide a sustainable way to enjoy the flavors of the harvest throughout the year. Whether you're making sauerkraut, kombucha, or classic dill pickles, the joy of creating these delicacies at home is as rewarding as the delicious results. Embrace the art of fermentation and pickling, and let your kitchen become a space for exploration, experimentation, and the joy of preserving flavors.

Chapter 8:

Off-Grid Communication and Technology

Introduction: Learning About Communication Outside Conventional Networks

In today's fast-changing world with lots of new technology, talking to each other has become really important in our everyday lives. While conventional networks like the internet, phone systems, and social media dominate the communication landscape, there exists a rich tapestry of alternative and unconventional methods that have been utilized across cultures and contexts. This introduction explores the fascinating realm of communication beyond traditional networks, delving into ancient practices, emerging technologies, and the diverse ways people connect and share information outside the mainstream channels.

The Landscape of Conventional Communication

In the 21st century, conventional communication has undergone a revolutionary transformation. The emergence of the smartphones, internet, and social media platforms has interconnected people worldwide, enabling instant communication, rapid information sharing, and seamless social interaction. However, this interconnectedness comes with its challenges, including issues of privacy, information overload, and dependence on centralized systems.

While conventional networks offer unprecedented reach and efficiency, the exploration of alternative communication methods becomes increasingly relevant in addressing the limitations and diversifying the ways people connect.

Ancient Wisdom and Traditional Communication

Before the age of the internet and smartphones, communities relied on ancient wisdom to communicate across distances and share information. This included various forms of signaling, such as smoke signals, drum beats, and semaphore flags. These methods were instrumental in conveying messages across challenging terrains or in circumstances where spoken words couldn't reach.

- **Smoke Signals:** Used by indigenous peoples, smoke signals involve creating distinct patterns of smoke to convey messages over long distances. Different patterns could communicate varying messages, such as warnings or celebrations.
- **Drum Communication:** African and Native American communities utilized drums for communication. The rhythm and beats could convey specific messages, and skilled drummers could transmit complex information over considerable distances.
- **Semaphore Flags:** Semaphore flags were employed in naval and military contexts to visually transmit messages using a system of flag positions. This method allowed for communication between ships and across battlefields.

These ancient methods showcase the human capacity for ingenuity in finding ways to bridge gaps and connect across distances, often in environments where traditional spoken language might fall short.

Emerging Technologies in Unconventional Communication

As technology continues to advance, new and unconventional methods of communication are emerging, providing alternatives to mainstream networks. These technologies leverage innovative approaches to connectivity and often prioritize decentralized, peer-to-peer communication.

1. **Mesh Networks:** Mesh networks are decentralized communication systems where each device in the network serves as a node, relaying data to other devices. This allows for communication even in areas with limited or no internet infrastructure.

2. **Radio Frequency (RF) Communication:** RF communication, including low-frequency radio waves, has been a traditional method, but emerging technologies are exploring its potential for local and community-based communication, particularly in disaster-stricken or remote areas.

3. **Bluetooth and Peer-to-Peer Apps:** Bluetooth technology enables devices to communicate directly with each other, bypassing the need for an internet connection. Peer-to-peer apps leverage this technology to facilitate communication in proximity, fostering local networks.

These emerging technologies exemplify the ongoing quest for decentralized and resilient communication systems, especially in scenarios where conventional networks might be unreliable or unavailable.

Challenges and Opportunities in Unconventional Communication

While unconventional communication methods offer diversity and resilience, they also present challenges. Ensuring widespread adoption, overcoming technological barriers, and addressing issues of accessibility remain critical considerations. Additionally, the cultural and contextual relevance of communication methods should be respected to avoid imposing foreign frameworks on diverse communities.

1. **Accessibility and Inclusivity:** Unconventional communication methods must prioritize accessibility, ensuring that diverse communities can adopt and benefit from these approaches. This includes considerations for people with disabilities and those in resource-limited environments.

2. **Technological Literacy:** The success of emerging technologies relies on the level of technological literacy within communities. Efforts to educate and empower individuals in using these tools play an important role in their effectiveness.

3. **Cultural Sensitivity:** Cultural context heavily influences communication. It's essential to approach unconventional communication with cultural sensitivity, recognizing and respecting diverse practices and traditions.

Navigating these challenges presents an opportunity for collaboration, innovation, and the co-creation of communication systems that are inclusive, resilient, and reflective of the diverse needs of global communities.

In the ever-evolving landscape of communication, exploring methods beyond conventional networks unveils a rich tapestry of human ingenuity, cultural diversity, and technological innovation. From ancient practices rooted in necessity to emerging technologies designed for resilience, each method contributes to the global conversation in its unique way.

Understanding communication outside traditional networks is not just about finding alternatives but also recognizing the cultural, social, and human dimensions inherent in how we connect. As we journey through this exploration, we embrace the diversity of voices, narratives, and expressions that weave together to create a vibrant and interconnected global community. This is an invitation to appreciate the myriad ways in which we communicate, learn from one another, and collectively contribute to the ever-evolving world.

Setting Up Off-Grid Internet and Wi-Fi Systems: Step by Step Project

Off-grid Internet and Wi-Fi systems are crucial for remote areas or emergency situations where traditional connectivity is unavailable. These projects focus on creating self-sustaining communication networks, often powered by renewable energy sources. Solar panels, wind turbines, or hand-crank generators provide the energy needed for routers and communication devices. Low-power and long-range Wi-Fi technologies are employed for connectivity.

Step 1: Assessing Your Location and Requirements

- **Evaluate Internet Availability:** Research available off-grid internet options in your area, such as satellite, cellular, or point-to-point wireless connections.
- **Determine Bandwidth Needs:** Assess your bandwidth requirements based on your internet usage, considering factors like web browsing, video streaming, and online communication.
- **Choose an Off-Grid Router:** Select a router that supports off-grid connectivity options, such as a cellular router or one compatible with satellite connections.

Step 2: Choosing Off-Grid Internet Options

- **Satellite Internet:** Consider satellite internet for wide coverage in remote areas. Choose a satellite provider and install a satellite dish, modem, and associated equipment.
- **Cellular Internet:** Explore cellular internet options. Choose a cellular provider, install a cellular router, and consider external antennas for improved signal strength.
- **Point-to-Point Wireless:** In cases where line-of-sight is possible, point-to-point wireless systems can be set up between locations for internet connectivity. Research suitable equipment and frequencies.

Step 3: Material List for Off-Grid Internet Setup

- **Off-Grid Router:** Choose a router compatible with your selected off-grid internet option.
- **Satellite Dish and Modem (if using satellite internet):** Purchase a satellite dish, modem, and related accessories from your chosen satellite provider.
- **Cellular Router (if using cellular internet):** Select a cellular router compatible with your chosen cellular provider.
- **External Antennas (if needed):** Consider external antennas to boost cellular signal strength.
- **Point-to-Point Wireless Equipment (if using this option):** Acquire the necessary equipment for point-to-point wireless connectivity, including antennas, radios, and mounting hardware.
- **Power Supply:** Choose a reliable power supply, such as solar panels with a charge controller and batteries, to ensure continuous off-grid operation.

Step 4: Designing the Off-Grid Wi-Fi Network

- **Plan Wi-Fi Coverage:** Determine the areas you need to cover with Wi-Fi and plan the placement of routers or access points accordingly.
- **Configure Wi-Fi Security:** Set up secure Wi-Fi encryption (WPA3 is recommended) to protect your network from unauthorized access.
- **Create SSIDs and Passwords:** Create unique SSIDs for your Wi-Fi networks and strong passwords to ensure network security.

- **Establish Guest Networks (optional):** If needed, set up separate guest networks to keep your main network secure.

Step 5: Installing and Configuring Off-Grid Internet Equipment

- **Satellite Internet Installation:** Follow the satellite provider's instructions to install the satellite dish, modem, and related equipment. Aim the dish for optimal signal reception.
- **Cellular Internet Installation:** Install the cellular router and external antennas if needed. Configure the router with the settings provided by your cellular provider.
- **Point-to-Point Wireless Setup:** If using point-to-point wireless, follow the manufacturer's guidelines to set up the antennas and configure the radios.
- **Connect Power Supply:** Connect the off-grid power supply to your internet equipment, ensuring a stable and reliable power source.

Step 6: Testing and Optimizing Connectivity

- **Check Signal Strength:** Verify signal strength for satellite or cellular connections. Adjust antenna placement or router location if needed.
- **Test Internet Speed:** Conduct speed tests to ensure your off-grid internet connection meets your bandwidth requirements.
- **Optimize Wi-Fi Coverage:** Adjust router or access point placement to optimize Wi-Fi coverage in your living space.
- **Secure Wi-Fi Network:** Double-check Wi-Fi security settings and make any necessary adjustments to enhance network security.

Step 7: Maintenance and Troubleshooting

- **Regular System Checks:** Periodically check your off-grid internet equipment for proper functioning. Ensure that all components are powered and connected.
- **Update Firmware and Software:** Stay up-to-date with firmware and software updates for your router or other off-grid internet equipment.
- **Troubleshoot Connectivity Issues:** If you experience connectivity issues, troubleshoot by checking signal strength, power supply, and any potential interference.

- **Monitor Data Usage (if applicable):** Keep an eye on your data usage, especially if you have limitations or costs associated with your off-grid internet plan.

By following these step-by-step instructions and considering the material list, you can establish a robust off-grid internet and Wi-Fi system tailored to your needs. Whether you're living in a remote location, a mobile setup, or simply seeking alternatives to traditional internet providers, this project empowers you to embrace connectivity off the grid.

Establishing A Reliable Emergency Communication System

A Reliable Emergency Communication System is crucial for no-grid survival. Establishing a network independent of traditional infrastructure ensures communication during crises. Utilizing radio frequencies or satellite technology, this project enables swift information exchange among community members. Portable, solar-powered communication devices with long battery life enhance resilience. Implementing simple, user-friendly interfaces ensures accessibility for all, promoting inclusivity in emergency situations. Regular drills and community education foster familiarity with the system, enhancing its effectiveness during real emergencies. This project aims to bridge communication gaps, providing a lifeline when conventional channels fail.

Step 1: Assessing Your Communication Needs

- **Identify Potential Risks:** Understand the types of emergencies or disasters common to your region, such as natural disasters, power outages, or public emergencies.
- **Define Communication Goals:** Clearly outline your communication goals, considering factors like family coordination, emergency alerts, and obtaining real-time information.
- **Account for Special Needs:** Consider the needs of all individuals in your household, including children, elderly family members, and individuals with specific medical requirements.

Step 2: Selecting Communication Channels

- **Primary Communication Channels:** Identify primary communication channels, such as mobile phones, landlines, or internet-based communication apps.
- **Backup Communication Channels:** Choose backup channels, including two-way radios, satellite phones, or other communication devices that operate independently of traditional infrastructure.
- **Community Alert Systems:** Register for community alert systems and stay informed about local emergency notification platforms.

Step 3: Acquiring Emergency Communication Tools

- **Two-Way Radios:** Invest in reliable two-way radios with sufficient range for your needs. Consider models with weather channels and emergency features.
- **Satellite Phones:** Acquire a satellite phone for communication in remote areas or during situations where cellular networks may be compromised.
- **Emergency Weather Radio:** Purchase a NOAA Weather Radio to receive real-time weather updates and emergency alerts.
- **Portable Power Sources:** Ensure access to portable power sources, such as power banks or solar chargers, to keep communication devices charged.

Step 4: Creating Emergency Contact Lists

- **Family Emergency Plan:** Create a comprehensive family emergency strategy encompassing contact details, designated meeting spots, and evacuation pathways.
- **Emergency Contact List:** Create a comprehensive emergency contact list with contact numbers for family members, neighbors, and local emergency services.
- **Medical Information:** Include essential medical information for each family member, such as allergies, medications, and emergency contacts.

Step 5: Establishing Communication Protocols

- **Check-In Procedures:** Define regular check-in procedures during emergencies to ensure the well-being and whereabouts of family members.
- **Code Words or Signals:** Establish code words or signals to convey specific messages without disclosing sensitive information.
- **Emergency Phrases:** Agree on key phrases to communicate urgency and priority messages.

Step 6: Testing and Familiarization

- **Regular System Tests:** Conduct regular tests of your emergency communication system to ensure all devices are functional.
- **Familiarize Family Members:** Educate all family members on the operation of communication devices and the family emergency plan.
- **Practice Drills:** Conduct emergency communication drills to simulate real-life scenarios and enhance preparedness.

Step 7: Storing Communication Equipment Securely

- **Waterproof Containers:** Store communication devices in waterproof containers to protect them from environmental factors.
- **Secure Locations:** Identify secure locations within your home or community to store communication tools, ensuring easy access during emergencies.

Step 8: Stay Informed and Updated

- **Emergency Information Sources:** Stay informed through reliable sources such as local news, weather apps, and official emergency alerts.
- **Community Networks:** Engage with local community networks and organizations to share information and resources.
- **Government Alerts:** Enable government alerts on your mobile phone to receive real-time emergency notifications.

Step 9: Continuous Improvement

- **Gather Feedback:** After emergencies or drills, gather feedback from family members to identify areas for improvement in your communication system.
- **Update Emergency Plans:** Consistently revisit and revise your family emergency plan and contact lists to ensure they accurately represent any alterations in your circumstances or contact details.
- **Adapt to New Technologies:** Stay informed about advancements in communication technologies and consider integrating new tools that enhance your emergency communication system.

Creating a reliable emergency communication system is an ongoing process that requires planning, preparation, and adaptability. By following these steps and considering the unique needs of your household or community, you can establish a resilient communication framework that enhances safety and coordination during challenging times.

Understanding Satellite Navigation and Mapping

In today's world, satellite navigation and mapping are important parts of our everyday lives. They help us find our way on roads, discover new places, and assist in responding to disasters. This guide delves into the intricacies of satellite navigation and mapping, exploring the technologies behind GPS (Global Positioning System), mapping applications, and the myriad ways these tools impact various aspects of our world.

Introduction to Satellite Navigation

- **Understanding GPS:** GPS is a system that uses satellites to help people find exactly where they are on Earth. There are a bunch of satellites flying around the Earth as part of this system.
- **GPS Components:** Satellites in space form the space segment, while GPS receivers on the ground make up the user segment. Ground control stations manage and maintain the satellites.
- **How GPS Works:** GPS receivers on Earth communicate with multiple satellites simultaneously. By triangulating signals from these satellites, the receiver calculates the user's exact location, considering factors like distance and time.

Applications of Satellite Navigation

1. **Navigation Systems:** GPS is commonly used in navigation for things like cars, ships, airplanes, and smartphones. It helps give directions and find the best route in real-time.

2. **Location-Based Services:** Mobile apps leverage GPS for location-based services, offering functionalities like finding nearby restaurants, tracking fitness activities, and geotagging photos.

3. **Precision Agriculture:** Farmers use GPS technology for precision agriculture, optimizing planting, harvesting, and resource management based on accurate location data.

4. **Emergency Response:** Emergency services rely on satellite navigation to coordinate responses during disasters, accidents, or search and rescue operations.

Mapping Technologies

1. **Geographic Information Systems (GIS):** GIS integrates spatial data with information, allowing users to analyze and visualize patterns, make informed decisions, and solve complex problems.

2. **Remote Sensing:** The process of remote sensing includes gathering information about the surface of the Earth from a distance, typically through the use of satellite photography. This data is crucial for mapping and monitoring changes in the environment.

3. **3D Mapping and Lidar:** Advanced mapping technologies incorporate Lidar (Light Detection and Ranging) to create detailed 3D maps, aiding in urban planning, infrastructure development, and environmental studies.

Mapping Applications

1. **Online Mapping Services:** Platforms like Google Maps, Apple Maps, and others provide interactive maps, turn-by-turn navigation, and information about points of interest.

2. **Cartography and Map Design:** Cartographers use satellite imagery and GIS to create detailed maps, combining artistic elements with accurate representation for various purposes.

3. **Disaster Management:** During disasters, mapping technologies play an important role in assessing damage, planning evacuation routes, and coordinating relief efforts.

Challenges and Future Developments

1. **Signal Interference:** GPS signals can be disrupted by factors like tall buildings, dense forests, or intentional interference, posing challenges to accurate navigation.

2. **Improved Accuracy:** Ongoing advancements aim to enhance GPS accuracy, with technologies like Differential GPS (DGPS) and Real-Time Kinematic (RTK) systems providing centimeter-level precision.

3. **Integration with Emerging Technologies:** Satellite navigation is increasingly integrated with emerging technologies like augmented reality (AR) and the Internet of Things (IoT) to create innovative and immersive experiences.

Ethical and Privacy Considerations

1. **Location Privacy:** The widespread use of location-based services raises concerns about individual privacy, leading to discussions about data protection and user consent.

2. **Security Risks:** As critical infrastructure relies on satellite navigation, there are concerns about potential security risks, including spoofing and jamming attacks.

Satellite navigation and mapping technologies have transformed the way we explore, navigate, and understand our world. From GPS guiding our daily commutes to advanced mapping applications aiding in disaster response, these technologies have become indispensable. As we navigate the future, ongoing developments and ethical considerations will shape how we harness the power of satellite navigation and mapping to create a more connected, informed, and resilient global community.

Chapter 9:

Health, Hygiene, And Natural Medicine

Introduction: Navigating Health and Wellness Challenges in Off-Grid Environments

In the pursuit of off-grid living, individuals and communities embark on a journey that disconnects them from traditional utilities and systems. While this lifestyle offers the allure of self-sufficiency and a closer connection to nature, it also presents unique health and wellness challenges. In this introduction, we delve into the intricacies of navigating well-being in off-grid environments, understanding the physical and mental aspects, and crafting strategies for a balanced and sustainable lifestyle.

The Allure and Realities of Off-Grid Living

Off-grid living is a conscious choice to disconnect from mainstream power, water, and communication systems, fostering a lifestyle deeply rooted in self-sufficiency. Whether nestled in a remote cabin, living in a sustainable community, or adopting a nomadic lifestyle, those embracing off-grid living seek a harmonious relationship with nature, reduced environmental impact, and a break from the fast-paced modern world.

However, this lifestyle choice is not without its challenges. Off-grid enthusiasts face unique obstacles related to health and wellness, necessitating creative solutions and a holistic approach to ensure a thriving life away from the conveniences of urban living.

Physical Well-being in Off-Grid Environments

1. Water Sourcing and Purification

Off-grid living often entails sourcing water from natural reservoirs, requiring robust purification methods. Clean water is fundamental for hydration, cooking, and sanitation, and individuals must implement effective filtration systems to mitigate health risks.

2. Sustainable Nutrition

Growing and sourcing food in off-grid environments necessitates a shift towards sustainable and often seasonal diets. Cultivating a diverse garden, practicing permaculture, and exploring alternative food sources become integral to ensuring a nutritionally balanced lifestyle.

3. Renewable Energy for Health Devices

Off-grid individuals rely on renewable energy sources such as solar or wind power. Ensuring a stable energy supply is crucial for powering health-related devices, refrigeration for medications, and medical equipment if needed.

Mental Wellness and Community Dynamics

1. Isolation and Community Support

Off-grid living can lead to physical isolation from mainstream society. While this solitude offers tranquility, it may pose mental health challenges. Establishing a supportive off-grid community or maintaining connections with like-minded individuals becomes vital for emotional well-being.

2. Adaptation to Nature's Rhythms

The off-grid lifestyle aligns with the natural rhythms of day and night, seasons, and weather patterns. Adapting to these cycles can positively impact mental health, fostering a deeper connection with the environment and promoting a more balanced lifestyle.

3. Mindful Technology Use

Off-grid living encourages a mindful approach to technology use. While digital devices might be limited, they can serve as tools for education, communication, and entertainment. Balancing technology with moments of unplugged serenity is key to mental wellness.

Healthcare Access and Preparedness

1. Off-Grid First Aid and Wellness Practices

Off-grid individuals often adopt a DIY approach to healthcare. Basic first aid skills, knowledge of herbal remedies, and wellness practices become essential for addressing common health issues in the absence of immediate medical assistance.

2. Emergency Communication Systems

Establishing reliable emergency communication systems is paramount. Satellite phones, two-way radios, and strategic community planning ensure that assistance can be sought in critical situations.

3. Preparedness for Remote Living

Off-grid dwellers must be prepared for medical emergencies. This includes having a well-equipped first aid kit, understanding evacuation procedures, and potentially investing in telemedicine services for remote consultations.

In navigating health and wellness challenges in off-grid environments, a holistic and proactive approach is fundamental. This involves embracing the symbiotic relationship with nature, adapting to sustainable nutrition practices, fostering mental resilience through community and connection, and ensuring preparedness for healthcare needs.

As individuals and communities venture into the uncharted territories of off-grid living, the journey becomes not just a quest for self-sufficiency but a profound exploration of balance, harmony, and well-being. By addressing the unique health challenges that come with this lifestyle, off-grid enthusiasts can truly cultivate a sustainable and enriching existence, living in harmony with nature while nurturing the most valuable asset—health.

Creating A Medicinal Herb Garden: Step by Step Project

A medicinal herb garden is a vital component of no-grid survival projects, offering self-sufficiency in healthcare. Cultivating various medicinal plants provides a renewable source of remedies for common ailments. Herbs like chamomile, lavender, and echinacea can be grown to alleviate stress, promote sleep, and boost the immune system. In a no-grid scenario, access to conventional medicine may be limited, making these herbs invaluable. Additionally, the garden fosters knowledge of herbalism, empowering individuals to harness nature's healing properties. With proper care, the medicinal herb garden ensures a sustainable supply of natural remedies, reducing dependence on external sources. This project not only enhances survival skills but also contributes to overall well-being, reinforcing the principle of resilience through self-reliance in challenging situations.

Step 1: Planning Your Medicinal Herb Garden

- **Select a Location:** Choose a sunny location with well-draining soil for your medicinal herb garden. Consider factors like sunlight exposure, proximity to water sources, and protection from harsh weather conditions.
- **Research Medicinal Herbs:** Identify medicinal herbs that thrive in your climate. Think about things like the kind of soil, the temperature, and how much water is needed. Common medicinal herbs include lavender, chamomile, echinacea, and calendula.
- **Design Your Garden Layout:** Plan the layout of your garden, organizing herbs based on their compatibility and growth habits. Put herbs that like the same amount of water and sunlight in the same group.

Step 2: Material List for Medicinal Herb Garden

- **Seeds or Seedlings:** Acquire seeds or seedlings of your chosen medicinal herbs. Consider purchasing from reputable nurseries or sourcing organic, non-GMO varieties.
- **Quality Soil and Compost:** Ensure you have high-quality soil with good drainage. Incorporate organic compost to enrich the soil with nutrients.

- **Garden Tools:** Gather essential garden tools, including a trowel, shovel, rake, and watering can.
- **Mulch:** Purchase organic mulch to help retain moisture, suppress weeds, and regulate soil temp.
- **Plant Markers:** Use plant markers or labels to identify each herb in your garden.

Step 3: Building the Garden Beds

- **Prepare the Soil:** Loosen the soil in your chosen area using a shovel or garden fork. Remove weeds, rocks, and debris. Amend the soil with compost for added fertility.
- **Create Garden Beds:** Define the boundaries of your garden beds. Use materials like wood, stone, or bricks to form raised beds if desired.
- **Apply Mulch:** Put a blanket of mulch on top of the soil. This helps with moisture retention and weed suppression.

Step 4: Planting Medicinal Herbs

- **Follow Planting Guidelines:** Refer to specific planting guidelines for each herb. Some herbs may require direct sowing, while others are best started indoors and transplanted.
- **Planting Depth and Spacing:** When planting seeds or young plants, make sure to put them in the ground at the right depth and distance as suggested. You can usually find these details on the seed packets or plant tags.
- **Watering:** Water the newly planted herbs thoroughly. Ensure consistent moisture, especially during the initial growth phase.

Step 5: Care and Maintenance

- **Weeding:** Regularly inspect your medicinal herb garden for weeds and remove them promptly to prevent competition for nutrients.
- **Pruning and Harvesting:** Practice regular pruning to encourage healthy growth. Harvest herbs when they reach their peak potency, usually before flowering.
- **Pest Control:** Monitor for pests and employ organic pest control methods if necessary. Companion planting with pest-repelling herbs is a natural strategy.
- **Fertilization:** Use organic fertilizers if needed. Follow guidelines for specific herbs and avoid over-fertilizing.

Step 6: Creating Herbal Remedies

- **Research Herbal Remedies:** Explore the medicinal properties of your herbs. Research and understand how to prepare herbal remedies such as teas, tinctures, or salves.
- **Harvesting for Remedies:** Harvest herbs at the right time for optimal potency. Dry herbs thoroughly before storing or using them in remedies.
- **Preservation:** Keep dried herbs in a cool and dark spot. Label containers with the herb name and harvest date.

Step 7: Enjoying Your Medicinal Herb Garden

- **Create a Relaxation Space:** Designate a cozy area within or near your herb garden for relaxation. This could include a bench, hammock, or seating arrangement.
- **Educational Signage:** Include educational signage to your garden, providing information about each herb's health benefits and uses.
- **Share with Community:** Share your knowledge and surplus herbs with the community. Consider organizing workshops or herb exchanges.

Creating a medicinal herb garden is not just a horticultural venture; it's a journey into the world of natural healing. By following these step-by-step instructions, you not only cultivate a vibrant garden but also empower yourself with the knowledge and resources to harness the medicinal properties of these herbs. Your garden becomes a haven for health, wellness, and connection to the ancient wisdom of herbal remedies. Enjoy the abundance of nature's pharmacy right in your backyard.

DIY Natural Hygiene Products: Recipes

Creating DIY natural hygiene products is a no-grid survival project that promotes self-sufficiency and sustainability. By making items like toothpaste, deodorant, and soap from readily available ingredients, individuals can reduce dependence on commercial products. This project not only ensures personal hygiene in off-grid scenarios but also minimizes environmental impact by avoiding harsh chemicals and excessive packaging. Ingredients like baking soda, coconut oil, and essential oils can be used to craft effective and eco-friendly alternatives. Additionally, acquiring the knowledge to produce these products empowers individuals with valuable skills for long-term self-reliance.

1. *Homemade Toothpaste*
Ingredients:

- 4 tbsps. of coconut oil
- 4 tbsps. of baking soda
- 1 tsp. of activated charcoal (optional for whitening)
- 10 drops of peppermint essential oil

Instructions:

1. Mix coconut oil, baking soda, and activated charcoal (if using) in a bowl.

2. Include peppermint essential oil and stir until thoroughly blended.

3. Transfer the mixture to a small jar with a lid.

4. Use as you would regular toothpaste, applying a small amount to your toothbrush.

2. *Natural Deodorant*
Ingredients:

- 3 tbsps. of coconut oil
- 3 tbsps. of shea butter
- 3 tbsps. of baking soda
- 2 tbsps. of arrowroot powder or cornstarch
- 10 drops of tea tree essential oil
- 10 drops of lavender essential oil

Instructions:

1. Use a double boiler to melt coconut oil and shea butter.

2. Take it off the heat and mix in baking soda and arrowroot powder.

3. Place tea tree and lavender essential oils and stir until everything is mixed together.

4. Pour the mixture into a clean, empty deodorant container or a small jar.

5. Allow it to cool and solidify before use.

3. *Homemade Shampoo*
Ingredients:

- 1 cup of liquid castile soap
- 1 cup of water
- 1 tbsp. of coconut oil
- 10 drops of your favorite essential oil (e.g., lavender, peppermint, tea tree)

Instructions:

1. The liquid castile soap and water should be combined in a bowl.

2. Include coconut oil and essential oil of your choice.

3. Give everything a good stir to blend all.

4. Transfer the mixture to a reusable shampoo bottle.

5. Shake well before each use, and apply to wet hair as you would with regular shampoo.

4. *DIY Body Wash*
Ingredients:

- 1 cup of liquid castile soap
- 1/4 cup of honey
- 1/4 cup of olive oil
- 30 drops of essential oil (e.g., citrus for a refreshing scent)

Instructions:

1. In a bowl, mix liquid castile soap, honey, and olive oil.

2. Include your chosen essential oil and stir until thoroughly blended.

3. Pour the mixture into a reusable body wash dispenser.

4. Shake well before each use, and enjoy the nourishing benefits of your DIY body wash.

5. *Natural Mouthwash*

Ingredients:

- 1 cup of distilled water
- 1 tbsp. of baking soda
- 10 drops of tea tree essential oil
- 10 drops of peppermint essential oil

Instructions:

1. Mix distilled water and baking soda in a glass container.

2. Include tea tree and peppermint essential oils and stir.

3. Store in a sealed container.

4. Shake well before each use, and swish a small amount in your mouth after brushing.

6. *DIY Lip Balm*

Ingredients:

- 2 tbsps. of coconut oil
- 1 tbsp. of shea butter
- 1 tbsp. of beeswax pellets
- 10 drops of your favorite essential oil (e.g., vanilla, citrus)

Instructions:

1. In your double boiler, melt coconut oil, shea butter, and beeswax together.

2. Take out from temp. and include essential oil.

3. Stir until thoroughly blended.

4. Place the mixture into small lip balm containers.

5. Let it cool and solidify before use.

Implementing Stress Management and Mindfulness Techniques

In today's busy world, stress is something we can't avoid. However, proactive stress management and mindfulness techniques can empower individuals to navigate life's challenges with resilience and balance. This section explores practical strategies to implement stress management and mindfulness techniques for a holistic approach to well-being.

Understanding Stress and Its Impact

- **Recognizing Stressors:** Identify the sources of stress in your life, including work pressures, personal relationships, or external factors. The first thing to do for effective management is to figure out why things happen in the first place.
- **Physiological Responses:** Understand how your body shows signs of stress, like a faster heartbeat, tense muscles, or difficulty sleeping. Awareness enables timely intervention.
- **Long-Term Effects:** Acknowledge the long-term impact of chronic stress on mental and physical health. Stress management is not just about immediate relief but about fostering long-term well-being.

Implementing Stress Management Techniques

1. **Regular Exercise:** Make sure to move your body regularly, whether it's going for a run, practicing yoga, or dancing. Exercise releases endorphins, the body's natural stress relievers.

2. **Breathing Exercises:** Practice deep breathing exercises to calm the nervous system. Techniques like diaphragmatic breathing or box breathing can be effective.

3. **Mindful Meditation:** Take some time to practice mindful meditation. Pay attention to what's happening right now, watch your thoughts without making judgments, and try to create a feeling of peace within yourself.

4. **Time Management:** Focus on what's most important, set achievable goals, and divide them into smaller tasks. Managing your time well helps you avoid feeling too stressed or overwhelmed.

5. **Healthy Lifestyle Choices:** Eat a variety of foods, drink enough water, and make sure to get enough sleep. These things are really important for keeping your body healthy and better able to handle stress.

Incorporating Mindfulness Techniques

1. **Mindful Awareness:** Cultivate mindful awareness in your daily activities. Pay attention to each moment, whether it's sipping tea, walking, or engaging in routine tasks.

2. **Mindful Eating:** Eating mindfully involves appreciating each bite and paying attention to the flavors and sensations of the food you are eating. Avoid distractions, and appreciate the nourishment your food provides.

3. **Mindful Listening:** Improve communication and relationships by practicing mindful listening. Fully engage in conversations without interrupting, and be present with the speaker.

4. **Gratitude Practice:** Keep a gratitude journal to focus on positive aspects of your life. Regularly acknowledging and appreciating the good moments fosters a positive mindset.

Creating a Mindful Environment

1. **Declutter Your Space:** Create a calm and organized living and working environment. Decluttering can contribute to a sense of order and peace.

2. **Digital Detox:** Set boundaries for digital devices. Allocate specific times for checking emails and social media to avoid constant connectivity-induced stress.

3. **Nature Connection:** Spend some time in the park. Connecting with nature, whether through activities such as gardening, going for a stroll in the park, or simply sitting outside, has been shown to have positive effects on mental health.

Fostering Emotional Intelligence

1. **Self-Reflection:** Engage in self-reflection to understand your emotions and reactions. Awareness of your emotional landscape allows for healthier responses to stressors.

2. **Empathy and Compassion:** Cultivate empathy and compassion, both for yourself and others. Understand that everyone faces challenges, and approach situations with understanding.

Seeking Professional Support

1. **Therapeutic Intervention:** If stress becomes overwhelming, consider seeking the support of a mental health professional. Therapy can provide tools and coping mechanisms tailored to your individual needs.

2. **Community and Social Connections:** Maintain strong social connections. Share your feelings with trusted friends or family members. Sometimes, the simple act of talking can be a powerful stress-relief tool.

By integrating stress management and mindfulness techniques into your daily life, you can cultivate a mindset of resilience and well-being. Remember that these practices are ongoing, and the key is consistency. As you embark on this journey, celebrate small victories, be patient with yourself, and embrace the transformative power of a mindful and resilient lifestyle.

Green Transportation and DIY Mechanics

Introduction: Initiating Independent and Sustainable Transportation Practices

In a world where transportation plays a pivotal role in our daily lives, exploring independent and sustainable alternatives becomes imperative for both personal well-being and the health of the planet. This introduction sets the stage for understanding the significance of embracing transportation practices that are not only independent but also sustainable. From reducing environmental impact to fostering self-reliance, this journey holds the potential to reshape our approach to getting from point A to point B.

The Dynamics of Modern Transportation

In the hustle and bustle of contemporary life, transportation has become synonymous with speed, convenience, and often, environmental challenges. Traditional modes of transportation, heavily reliant on fossil fuels, contribute significantly to air pollution, climate change, and dependency on centralized systems. This has led individuals to reconsider their choices, seeking ways to navigate the world that align with principles of sustainability, independence, and environmental consciousness.

Rising Interest in Independent Transportation

A growing interest in independent transportation is witnessed as individuals seek alternatives that empower them with control over their commuting experiences. From bicycles and electric scooters to compact electric vehicles, the desire for autonomy in travel choices is reshaping urban landscapes and personal preferences. This shift signifies not just a mode of movement but a conscious decision to reclaim personal agency and reduce one's ecological footprint.

The Urgency of Sustainable Practices

As the impacts of climate change become more pronounced, there is an increasing urgency to adopt sustainable transportation practices. Sustainable transportation involves choices that minimize environmental harm, promote energy efficiency, and reduce reliance on non-renewable resources. Embracing such practices is not just a lifestyle choice; it is a collective responsibility to protect the planet for current and future generations.

Navigating the Contents Ahead

This guide explores a spectrum of independent and sustainable transportation practices, ranging from eco-friendly vehicles to alternative modes of commuting. Each chapter delves into practical strategies, considerations, and step-by-step instructions for integrating these practices into daily life. From electric bicycles to carpooling, the journey ahead offers insights that cater to various preferences, budgets, and lifestyles.

Empowering Individuals and Communities

The quest for independent and sustainable transportation is not just an individual endeavor; it has the potential to transform communities. By embracing alternatives that prioritize environmental responsibility and self-sufficiency, individuals contribute to a broader shift in societal norms. Communities that endorse and implement sustainable transportation practices stand as beacons of change, fostering a collective consciousness that transcends personal choice.

Initiating independent and sustainable transportation practices is a multifaceted journey—one that involves personal choices, community engagement, and a commitment to environmental stewardship. As we embark on this exploration, let us consider the transformative power of our decisions and their ripple effects on the world around us. By taking steps towards greener, more independent transportation, we not only enhance our quality of life but also contribute to building a sustainable and resilient future for generations to come.

Building and Maintaining A Solar-Powered Electric Vehicle: Step by Step Project

A solar-powered electric vehicle (EV) combines sustainable energy with mobility, offering a self-sufficient solution for off-grid survival. The vehicle integrates solar panels on its exterior, harnessing sunlight to charge its electric battery. This reduces reliance on conventional charging stations and minimizes the environmental impact. In a survival context, it ensures continued transportation even in remote areas where traditional fuel sources might be scarce. The solar EV serves as a versatile power source, capable of supplying energy to essential appliances or acting as an emergency power station. Its grid-independent nature makes it ideal for navigating unpredictable scenarios, providing a reliable means of transportation and power generation. This project promotes sustainability, resilience, and adaptability, embodying a holistic approach to off-grid living.

Step 1: Planning Your Solar-Powered EV

- **Vehicle Selection:** Choose a suitable electric vehicle or convert an existing gasoline vehicle to an electric one. Consider factors like weight, aerodynamics, and space for solar panels.
- **Solar Panel Calculation:** Calculate the energy requirements and determine the surface area available for solar panels on your vehicle. Consider the daily mileage, battery capacity, and charging needs.
- **Battery Selection:** Choose high-quality lithium-ion batteries with sufficient capacity to store solar energy. The battery bank's capacity should align with your vehicle's energy consumption.

Step 2: Material List for Solar-Powered EV

- **Electric Vehicle:** Select an electric vehicle or a gasoline vehicle for conversion.
- **Solar Panels:** Purchase high-efficiency solar panels with a sufficient output for your energy needs.
- **Charge Controller:** Obtain a solar charge controller for the purpose of managing the energy transfer from the solar panels to the batteries.

- **Battery Bank:** Invest in lithium-ion batteries with the required capacity for storing solar energy.
- **Inverter:** Choose an inverter to convert DC power from the batteries to AC power for the electric motor.
- **Electric Motor:** If converting a gasoline vehicle, obtain an electric motor suitable for your vehicle's weight and size.
- **Wiring and Connectors:** Gather appropriate wiring, connectors, and fuses to create a safe and efficient electrical system.
- **Mounting Hardware:** Acquire sturdy mounting hardware to secure the solar panels to the vehicle roof.

Step 3: Installing Solar Panels on Your EV

- **Roof Preparation:** Ensure the vehicle roof is clean and well-prepared for solar panel installation.
- **Mounting Solar Panels:** Attach solar panels to the roof using the mounting hardware. Consider aerodynamics and ensure a secure fit.
- **Wiring Setup:** Connect the solar panels in series or parallel, depending on the voltage requirements. Connect the wiring to the solar charge controller.

Step 4: Installing the Electrical System

- **Battery Bank Installation:** Install the lithium-ion battery bank in a secure location within the vehicle. Ensure proper ventilation and cooling.
- **Charge Controller Connection:** Connect the solar charge controller to the battery bank and solar panels. Follow the manufacturer's guidelines for proper wiring.
- **Inverter Installation:** Install the inverter and connect it to the battery bank. Ensure the inverter is capable of handling the load from the electric motor.
- **Electric Motor Integration:** If converting a gasoline vehicle, remove the internal combustion engine and install the electric motor. Connect the motor to the inverter.

Step 5: Testing and Calibration

- **System Testing:** Perform comprehensive testing on the complete system, encompassing evaluations of solar panel performance, battery charging capabilities, and electric motor functionality.

- **Calibration:** Calibrate the charge controller and inverter settings to optimize energy conversion and utilization.

Step 6: Maintenance and Optimization

- **Regular Inspections:** Conduct routine inspections of the solar panels, wiring, and electrical components to identify and address any issues promptly.
- **Battery Maintenance:** Monitor battery health and charge levels. Perform regular maintenance and replace batteries when needed.
- **Efficiency Optimization:** Explore ways to optimize the efficiency of your solar-powered EV, such as adjusting panel angles for maximum sunlight exposure.
- **Software Updates:** Stay updated on the latest software updates available for your electric motor, inverter, and charge controller to ensure optimal performance and functionality. Update as necessary to access performance improvements.

Building and maintaining a solar-powered electric vehicle is a transformative journey toward sustainable transportation. By harnessing the power of the sun, you not only reduce your carbon footprint but also contribute to a cleaner and greener future. As you embark on this eco-friendly adventure, remember that every mile driven is a step toward a more sustainable and resilient world.

Bicycle Maintenance and DIY Repairs

Cycling is not just a mode of transportation or a form of exercise; it's a way of life. To ensure your bicycle remains a reliable companion on your journeys, understanding maintenance and mastering do-it-yourself (DIY) repairs is crucial. This section takes you through the essentials of bicycle maintenance, empowering you to keep your bike in top-notch condition and handle common repairs with confidence.

Step 1: Basic Tools and Equipment

- **Bicycle Repair Stand:** Invest in a bicycle repair stand to elevate your bike, making it easier to work on different components.
- **Basic Toolkit:** Acquire a toolkit with essential tools, including screwdrivers, wrenches, Allen keys, and a chain breaker.

- **Lubricants and Cleaners:** Purchase bicycle-specific lubricants and degreasers for maintaining the chain, gears, and other moving parts.
- **Tire Pump:** Have a reliable tire pump with a pressure gauge for maintaining optimal tire pressure.

Step 2: Cleaning Your Bike

- **Hose or Bucket of Water:** Rinse off dirt and grime using a hose or a bucket of water. Be mindful not to use high-pressure water directly on sensitive components.
- **Bike-Friendly Cleaner:** Use a bike-specific cleaner to scrub the frame, wheels, and other parts. Avoid harsh chemicals that may damage paint or components.
- **Soft Brushes and Cloths:** Use soft brushes and cloths to scrub hard-to-reach areas and remove stubborn dirt.
- **Chain Cleaning Device:** Employ a chain cleaning device with degreaser to thoroughly clean the chain.

Step 3: Checking and Adjusting the Brakes

- **Inspect Brake Pads:** Examine brake pads for wear. Replace them if the grooves are shallow or if there are any signs of damage.
- **Adjust Brake Cable Tension:** Use the barrel adjuster on the brake caliper or brake lever to fine-tune cable tension. Ensure the brake pads engage simultaneously.
- **Center the Brake Pads:** If your brakes are misaligned, loosen the brake caliper bolts, center the pads on the rim, and retighten the bolts.
- **Test and Fine-Tune:** Test the brakes for responsiveness and adjust as necessary. Make sure the levers don't bottom out on the handlebars.

Step 4: Maintaining the Gears and Drivetrain

- **Check Gear Shifting:** Shift through all gears to ensure smooth and accurate shifting. Adjust cable tension using barrel adjusters if needed.
- **Lubricate the Chain:** Apply a bicycle-specific lubricant to the chain, ensuring even coverage. Wipe off excess lubricant with a clean rag.
- **Inspect the Cassette and Chainrings:** Examine the cassette and chainrings for wear. Replace if teeth are visibly worn.
- **Adjust Derailleurs:** Fine-tune derailleur adjustments using limit screws and barrel adjusters. Ensure the chain runs smoothly on all gears.

Step 5: Checking and Adjusting Tire Pressure

- **Use a Pressure Gauge:** Check tire pressure regularly using a pressure gauge. Refer to the recommended pressure range imprinted on the tire sidewall.
- **Inflate or Deflate:** Inflate or deflate the tires to reach the optimal pressure.
- **Inspect for Damage:** Check the tires for cuts, bulges, or embedded objects. Replace damaged tires to prevent blowouts.

Step 6: Inspecting and Adjusting Bearings

- **Wheel Bearings:** Spin each wheel and feel for any roughness or wobbling. Adjust or replace wheel bearings as needed.
- **Headset Bearings:** Check for play in the headset by holding the front brake and rocking the bike forward and backward. Adjust headset bearings if necessary.
- **Bottom Bracket Bearings:** Grasp the crank arms and rock them side to side. If there's play, adjust or replace bottom bracket bearings.

Step 7: Securing Bolts and Nuts

- **Tighten Loose Bolts:** Inspect all bolts and nuts on your bike. Tighten any that may have loosened due to vibrations during riding.
- **Use a Torque Wrench:** For critical components like the stem, handlebars, and seatpost, use a torque wrench to ensure proper tightness without over-torquing.

Step 8: Suspension Maintenance (if applicable)

- **Check Suspension Sag:** Adjust suspension sag according to your weight. Refer to the manufacturer's guidelines for the recommended sag percentages.
- **Inspect Seals and Lubricate:** Check suspension seals for leaks and lubricate stanchions with appropriate suspension oil.

Conclusion: Enjoying a Smooth Ride

Consistent upkeep and self-made fixes for your bicycle not only prolong its lifespan but also enhance safety and make your riding experience more enjoyable. By following these step-by-step instructions and dedicating time to caring for your bike, you'll ensure that it remains a reliable and efficient means of transportation or recreation. Whether you're a casual rider or a seasoned cyclist, the rewards of a well-maintained bicycle are numerous, from enhanced performance to the satisfaction of a smooth and trouble-free ride.

Conclusion

As we conclude this transformative journey into the world of off-grid living, it's time to reflect on the lessons learned, the challenges overcome, and the path towards future self-sufficiency and sustainability. The off-grid lifestyle is not merely a departure from mainstream living; it's a conscious choice to embrace a more harmonious and sustainable way of coexisting with our environment.

Reflecting on The Off-Grid Journey

- **Embracing Independence:** The decision to embrace an off-grid lifestyle reflects a desire for independence and self-reliance. Through harnessing alternative energy sources, cultivating food, and implementing sustainable practices, individuals embark on a journey towards a more autonomous way of living.
- **Navigating Challenges:** The off-grid journey is not without its challenges. From establishing reliable water sources to generating power sustainably, each hurdle provides an opportunity for learning and adaptation. Overcoming these challenges fosters resilience and a deeper connection with the environment.
- **Environmental Stewardship:** Off-grid living inherently promotes environmental stewardship. By minimizing reliance on conventional utilities and incorporating eco-friendly practices, individuals contribute to the conservation of natural resources, reduction of carbon footprints, and preservation of biodiversity.
- **Connection to Nature:** Living off-grid brings individuals closer to nature. The daily rhythm aligns with natural cycles, fostering a profound connection to the changing seasons, weather patterns, and the diverse ecosystem that surrounds. This connection becomes a source of inspiration and spiritual nourishment.
- **Resourcefulness and Innovation:** Off-grid living cultivates resourcefulness and innovation. The need to find solutions for energy production, water conservation, and sustainable agriculture encourages creativity. DIY projects, renewable energy systems, and innovative water management solutions become integral parts of this lifestyle.

- **Community Building:** The off-grid community, though scattered across diverse landscapes, shares a common thread of self-sufficiency and sustainability. Interactions with like-minded individuals, whether in person or through virtual platforms, create a supportive network that shares knowledge, experiences, and encouragement.

Planning for Future Self-Sufficiency and Sustainability

- **Continuous Learning:** The off-grid journey is a continuous learning process. Staying informed about advancements in sustainable technologies, permaculture practices, and alternative energy solutions ensures ongoing improvement and adaptation to changing needs.
- **Sustainable Food Systems:** Future self-sufficiency involves enhancing and diversifying sustainable food systems. This may include expanding gardens, incorporating permaculture principles, and exploring innovative methods such as aquaponics or vertical farming to ensure a consistent and varied food supply.
- **Advancements in Energy Independence:** As technology evolves, so do the opportunities for energy independence. Continued exploration of advancements in solar, wind, and hydroelectric systems allows for enhanced efficiency and reliability in off-grid energy production.
- **Water Management and Conservation:** Planning for future self-sufficiency requires a keen focus on water management and conservation. Implementing rainwater harvesting systems, improving water storage capacity, and exploring water-efficient technologies contribute to long-term sustainability.
- **Technological Integration:** Integrating smart and sustainable technologies can enhance off-grid living. From efficient energy storage solutions to IoT-based monitoring for resource management, embracing technological advancements complements the traditional aspects of self-sufficiency.
- **Advocacy and Community Involvement:**
- Building a sustainable future goes beyond individual efforts. Advocacy for off-grid living, sustainable practices, and environmental conservation can create positive change at a broader level. Engaging with local communities and policymakers fosters a supportive environment for off-grid initiatives.

- **Resilience Planning:** Future self-sufficiency involves planning for resilience in the face of unforeseen challenges. This includes developing contingency plans for extreme weather events, economic fluctuations, and other factors that may impact off-grid living.

In conclusion, the off-grid journey is not a destination but a dynamic and evolving lifestyle that champions self-sufficiency, sustainability, and environmental harmony. Reflecting on the lessons learned, the triumphs celebrated, and the challenges surmounted, it becomes evident that off-grid living is a conscious choice to create a sustainable tomorrow.

As we plan for the future, the principles ingrained in the off-grid lifestyle serve as beacons guiding us towards a more harmonious relationship with the planet. By embracing continuous learning, sustainable food systems, advancements in energy independence, water management, technological integration, advocacy, and resilience planning, individuals on the off-grid path contribute to a collective effort for a sustainable and resilient global community.

The off-grid journey is a testament to the transformative power of individual choices. Each solar panel, rainwater harvesting system, and permaculture garden becomes a small yet significant step towards a future where humanity coexists with nature in balance. As we continue to navigate this journey, let us carry forward the lessons of self-sufficiency, community building, and environmental stewardship, ensuring that the path to a sustainable tomorrow is one that we collectively tread with purpose and dedication.

Appendix

Resource Directory: Tools, Supplies, And Contacts

1. Tools and Supplies

Tool Suppliers:

Harbor Freight Tools

- Website: Harbor Freight Tools
- Contact: 1-800-444-3353

Home Depot

- Website: Home Depot
- Contact: 1-800-466-3337

Solar Equipment Providers:

Renogy

- Website: Renogy
- Contact: 1 (909) 287 7111

Goal Zero

- Website: Goal Zero
- Contact: 1-888-794-6250

Gardening and Permaculture Tools:

Johnny's Selected Seeds

- Website: Johnny's Selected Seeds
- Contact: 1-877-564-6697

Permaculture Tools

- Website: Permaculture Tools

Water Solutions:

Rainwater Harvesting Systems:

The Tank Depot

- Website: [The Tank Depot](#)
- Contact: (800) 573-6771

Bushman USA

- Website: [Bushman USA](#)
- Contact: (866) 920-TANK (8265)

Water Storage Tanks:

Plastic-Mart

- Website: [Plastic-Mart](#)
- Contact: 1-866-310-2556

Rain Harvesting Supplies

- Website: [Rain Harvesting Supplies](#)
- Contact: 1-877-331-7008

Renewable Energy Components:

Wind Turbine Providers:

Northern Tool + Equipment

- Website: [Northern Tool + Equipment](#)
- Contact: 1-800-221-0516

WindEnergy7

- Website: [WindEnergy7](#)
- Contact: 1-800-949-7474

2. *Building Materials*
Eco-Friendly Building Supplies:

Green Building Supply

- Website: [Green Building Supply](#)
- Contact: 855-496-0828

EcoBuilding Bargains

- Website: [EcoBuilding Bargains](#)
- Contact: 1-413-788-6900

Glossary of Key Terms and Concepts

Advocacy: The act of promoting or supporting a cause, such as off-grid living, through public awareness and policy influence.

Aquaponics: Aquaponics is an environmentally sustainable farming technique that merges aquaculture, which involves fish farming, with hydroponics, which involves growing plants in water. These two practices work synergistically within a symbiotic environment.

Biodiversity: The vast range and dynamic nature of life on Earth encompass the diversity of species, ecosystems, and genetic variations within species.

Battery Bank: A collection of interconnected batteries used to store electrical energy generated from renewable sources for later use.

Composting: The decomposition of organic material into a nutrient-rich soil conditioner, promoting recycling and reducing waste.

DIY (Do-It-Yourself): The practice of creating, building, or repairing things independently, without the direct assistance of professionals or experts.

Eco-Friendly Building Supplies: Materials and products that have minimal environmental impact in terms of production, use, and disposal.

Environmental Stewardship: The responsible management and care of the environment, ensuring its health and sustainability for current and future generations.

Greywater: Greywater refers to the wastewater generated from various domestic activities, such as laundry, dishwashing, and bathing. It specifically excludes toilet waste, as that is categorized separately as blackwater.

Hydroelectric System: A system that generates electricity by capturing energy from flowing or falling water.

Inverter: A device responsible for converting direct current (DC) electricity generated by batteries into alternating current (AC), suitable for powering household appliances.

IoT (Internet of Things): A network comprised of interconnected devices capable of communication and data-sharing, often employed for monitoring and control purposes.

Micro-Hydroelectric Power System: A small-scale hydroelectric system designed to generate electricity by harnessing the energy of flowing water.

Off-Grid Community: A group of individuals or families living independently from traditional utilities, often sharing knowledge and resources to foster sustainability.

Off-Grid Internet: Establishing internet connectivity through alternative means, such as satellite or wireless technologies, independent of traditional providers.

Off-Grid Living: A lifestyle that operates independently from public utilities, relying on self-sustaining practices for energy, water, and waste management.

Permaculture: An approach to designing and maintaining agricultural systems that mimic the relationships found in natural ecosystems, promoting sustainability and biodiversity.

Rainwater Harvesting: Rainwater collection and storage, commonly done using tanks or barrels, involves gathering precipitation for future use.

Renewable Energy: The utilization of energy derived from sources that naturally replenish within a human timescale, such as sunlight, wind, rain, tides, waves, and geothermal heat.

Renewable Energy Incentives: Financial benefits or subsidies provided by governments to encourage the adoption of renewable energy sources.

Resilience Planning: The process of developing strategies and preparations to withstand and recover from unforeseen challenges or crises.

Resourcefulness: The ability to find quick and clever ways to overcome challenges and solve problems using available resources.

Solar Charge Controller: A device designed to regulate the voltage and current from solar panels, preventing overcharging of batteries.

Solar Panel: A technology that converts sunlight into electricity by capturing and converting solar radiation.

Solar Water Distillation: A process that uses solar energy to evaporate water, leaving impurities behind, and then condenses the vapor to produce clean water.

Sustainable Agriculture: Farming practices that prioritize environmental health, biodiversity, and long-term soil fertility.

Water Storage Tanks: Containers designed to store and manage water collected from rainwater harvesting or other sources.

Wind Turbine: A device that operates by converting the kinetic energy from the wind into electrical power through the rotation of turbine blades connected to a generator.

Quick Reference Guide: Off-Grid Project Checklists

Embarking on off-grid projects requires meticulous planning and execution. These quick-reference checklists are designed to streamline your projects, ensuring that you cover essential aspects for a successful off-grid endeavor. Refer to these checklists for each phase of your projects to stay organized and efficient.

1. Off-Grid Living Essentials Checklist:

Energy:

- Assess energy needs.

- Choose renewable energy sources (solar, wind, hydro).

- Calculate solar panel or wind turbine capacity.

- Select and purchase batteries.

- Install solar panels or wind turbine.

Water:

- Identify water sources.

- Implement rainwater harvesting system.

- Install water storage tanks.

- Set up greywater recycling system.

Shelter:

- Choose eco-friendly building materials.

- Plan for insulation and energy efficiency.

- [ ] Install alternative heating and cooling systems.

- [ ] Consider passive cooling techniques.

2. Off-Grid Garden and Permaculture Checklist:

Gardening:

- [ ] Select suitable crops for the climate.

- [ ] Prepare and enrich the soil.

- [ ] Implement raised bed or container gardening.

- [ ] Install a drip irrigation system.

Permaculture:

- [ ] Design permaculture zones on your property.

- [ ] Implement companion planting for pest control.

- [ ] Establish a composting system.

- [ ] Integrate livestock or poultry for symbiotic relationships.

3. Off-Grid Energy Systems Checklist:

Solar Energy:

- [ ] Choose solar panels with optimal efficiency.

- [ ] Install solar charge controller.

- [ ] Set up the battery bank.

- [ ] Connect the inverter for AC power.

Wind Energy:

☐ Select an appropriate wind turbine.

☐ Install a charge controller for wind energy.

☐ Connect the wind turbine to the battery bank.

☐ Integrate the inverter for AC power.

Hydroelectric Energy:

☐ Assess the feasibility of a micro-hydro system.

☐ Choose suitable hydro system components.

☐ Install the hydroelectric system.

☐ Connect to the battery bank and inverter.

4. Off-Grid Water Solutions Checklist:

Rainwater Harvesting:

☐ Install a rainwater collection system.

☐ Set up first flush diverters.

☐ Connect gutters and downspouts.

☐ Install a filtration system.

Greywater Recycling:

☐ Identify greywater sources.

☐ Set up a greywater filtration system.

- ☐ Design a distribution system for greywater.

- ☐ Integrate greywater into garden irrigation.

5. Off-Grid Communication and Internet Checklist:

Communication:

- ☐ Explore alternative communication methods (walkie-talkies, ham radios).

- ☐ Set up an emergency communication plan with neighbors.

- ☐ Learn basic signaling techniques.

Internet:

- ☐ Research off-grid internet solutions (satellite, wireless).

- ☐ Install off-grid internet equipment.

- ☐ Set up a reliable Wi-Fi system.

6. Off-Grid Health and Wellness Checklist:

Medicinal Herb Garden:

- ☐ Choose medicinal herbs suited for your climate.

- ☐ Plan and design a medicinal herb garden.

- ☐ Plant and maintain the herb garden.

- ☐ Learn about herbal remedies and their uses.

Stress Management:

- ☐ Implement stress management techniques.

☐ Create a designated relaxation space.

☐ Practice mindfulness and meditation.

7. Off-Grid Transportation Checklist:

Solar-Powered Electric Vehicle:

☐ Choose or convert a suitable vehicle.

☐ Install solar panels on the vehicle.

☐ Set up a charging station.

☐ Maintain and optimize the solar-powered vehicle.

Bicycle Maintenance:

☐ Regularly check and maintain your bicycle.

☐ Learn basic bicycle repair techniques.

☐ Keep essential bicycle maintenance tools.

These checklists are designed to serve as a foundation for your off-grid projects. Modify and customize them based on your specific needs and the unique characteristics of your off-grid lifestyle. Regularly revisit and update these checklists to ensure ongoing success and sustainability in your off-grid endeavors.